Issa and Being Human: Haiku Portraits of Early Modern Japan

David G. Lanoue

Copyright © 2017 by David G. Lanoue

HaikuGuy.com

New Orleans, Louisiana, USA

All rights reserved.

ISBN-10: 0991284054
ISBN-13: 978-0991284054

The cover art shows a sketch of Issa from *Kokon haijin hyaku kusho* (1818).

Issa and Being Human: Haiku Portraits of Early Modern Japan

FOR ALICE

TABLE OF CONTENTS

Introduction: Remarkable or So-so? 6

Chapter 1. Children. 12

Chapter 2. Farmers. 31

Chapter 3. Priests 51

Chapter 4. Samurai 69

Chapter 5. Artisans and Merchants 84

Chapter 6. Entertainers 105

Chapter 7. Prostitutes 121

Chapter 8. Beggars, Outcastes, Thieves 138

Chapter 9. The Old 161

Conclusion: The Promise of Poppies 183

Appendix: More People Portraits by Issa 187

Notes 217

Works Cited 225

About the Author 229

INTRODUCTION: Remarkable or So-so?

In 1811 Japanese poet Kobayashi Issa (1763-1828) composed the following poem.

なかなかに人と生れて秋の暮 [1]
naka-naka ni hito to umarete aki no kure

quite remarkable
being born human . . .
autumn dusk

After writing it in his journal, *Waga haru shū* ("My Spring Collection"), he recopied it in six other texts, an exceedingly rare occurrence for Issa. This one-breath verse—what the poet would have labeled *haikai* but later generations came to know as "haiku"—begins with an enigmatic opening phrase: *naka-naka ni* なかなかに ("remarkable"), challenging readers to contemplate and imagine for themselves what might be remarkable about being born human. This challenge to imagine seems almost urgent in light of Issa's word-for-word inclusion of the poem in seven texts. Perhaps, therefore, it behooves readers to take a time reflecting on the question posed: What exactly *is* remarkable about human existence?

Since the poetic art of haiku involves imagery more than abstract argument, one needs to pay very close attention to a haiku's images and the often interesting juxtapositions that this imagery can create. Here, Issa pairs the wonder of human birth with the seasonal image of "autumn dusk." The phrase, *aki no kure* 秋の暮, denotes both an evening of autumn and the end or "dusk" of autumn as a season: the last evening before winter's first morning. Literally, Issa is saying that he is nearing the end of a year while, at the same time, he suggests on a symbolic level that he also is approaching his life's end. One juxtaposition in the haiku, then, is that of birth and death. Birth implies light, while death implies a cold, wintry darkness. Within the world of the haiku's imagery, an important first clue about Issa's understanding of the nature of human life thus emerges: it is temporary. Part of his understanding of the meaning of being human might therefore involve the preciousness of an existence in which people enjoy the light of day and consciousness for such a brief time . . . before winter and death.

A closer look at Issa's word choice casts even more light on the haiku, and raises more questions. The pivotal expression at the heart of the poem, *naka-naka ni*, which I translate here as "remarkable," can indeed denote "remarkable," "excellent," "wonderful," or "very good." However, because the word *naka* (中) literally means "middle," the phrase *naka-naka ni* might equally signify the condition of being in a middle state: not great, not terrible . . . something akin to the folksy English expression, "fair to middling."[2] If we read *naka-naka ni* in this way, Issa's haiku takes a radically different form in English translation:

> just so-so
> being born human . . .
> autumn dusk

This interpretation of *naka-naka ni* in a poem written by Issa is somewhat appealing, since it accords with the poet's love for humorous irony. Despite the popular belief in the good fortune of being born human, he might mischievously be suggesting that it is really only, in his view, a "so-so" existence. Eight years later, in 1819, he employs similar language—and a similar ironic reversal of expectations—in a famous poem about New Year's Day, the titular haiku of his journal for that year, *Oraga haru* ("My Spring").

目出度さもちう位也おらが春 (*IZ* 1819; 1.29)
medetasa mo chū kurai nari oraga haru

my "Happy New Year!"
about average . . .
my spring

Issa describes his New Year's felicity as merely *chū kurai* ちう位, "about average," *chū* being another reading of the kanji *naka*—"middle"—thus expressing, with deadpan humor, his surprising lack of rapture at this normally rapturous time. His countrymen rejoice on the year's most propitious day: a time for both national and natural renewal, since New Year's Day in the old Japanese calendar was not only the first day of a new imperial year but also the first day of spring. Nevertheless, Issa reports that his day is only "about average" or, as his language might also be translated, "just so-so." Returning to the "being born human" haiku, Issa's meaning here could be similarly, cantankerously ironic, claiming that human existence, far from being remarkable, is in fact only "so-so."

An investigation of a haiku's context, which can include not only the broad context of Japanese history and culture but also the more specific context of Issa's biography, can also assist in the decoding of its meaning(s). This particular poem evokes no specific episode or theme in Issa's life story[3], but its position on the page of his journal is possibly revealing. It appears first in *Waga haru shū* sandwiched between the following two verses about animal existence.

はつ雁やあてにして来る庵の畠 (1811; *IZ* 6.31)
hatsu kari ya ate ni shite kuru io no hata

autumn's first geese
hitting the mark . . .
field by my hut

牛の子の旅に立也秋の風 (1811; *IZ* 6.31)
ushi no ko no tabi ni tatsu nari aki no ame

the calf begins
his journey . . .
autumn rain

All three haiku have autumn settings. In the first, migrating geese descend to gather in a field by a hut, which could belong to Issa (hence I translate it here as "my hut," though it also could be rendered, more objectively, as "the hut"). The images of geese and a garden suggest a deep connection: a bird-human relationship. The geese alight to feed in this field perhaps every year, every autumn, implying a comforting regularity of nature's cycles in which the garden's owner, by planting and tending his plants, partici-pates—though, one presumes, unwillingly. The other haiku, appearing after the one about being born human, returns to a contemplation of animal existence: the image of a calf beginning a journey in autumn rain. The calf has been sold and now is being led away, forever, from his or her mother. The image becomes even more pathetic and poignant if we take into account Issa's loss of his own mother in early childhood and his decision to leave an unhappy, cruel stepmother-dominated home at age fourteen.[4]

In his journal, Issa's autumn haiku about the remarkableness or averageness of human birth appears between these two autumn poems about animal existence: a light-hearted scene of returning, scavenging geese and a more somber one about a departing calf. In the first poem, being born human might mean that one will live a life of participation in nature's cycles alongside his or her fellow creatures. In the third poem, being born human might mean that one will develop emotional intelligence and feel compassion for one's fellow creatures. Sensing a connection to the natural world and imagining what other beings are feeling might indeed be understood as remarkable, essentially human, abilities. However, if one chooses to read *naka-naka ni* as "just so-so," Issa might be making no special claim about the specialness of human existence. The poem, in the context of his journal, might simply be saying that being born human or wild goose or cow is all equal, all essentially one in the same. In Issa's Buddhist vision of the universe, articulated in thousands of verses, he repeatedly affirms a belief in reincarnation, such that "being born human" is just one possible existential option among many. Although most pious Buddhists may consider human birth as remarkable in the sense of being a lucky occurrence, happening against long odds; Issa, a born iconoclast, likes to portray human life as no better, and often worse, than non-human animals.[5] Rebirth as a human being lies just a step below rebirth as a heavenly being in the contemporary "Six Ways" (*roku dō* 六道) schema of reincarnation, an exceedingly fortunate incarnation according to the majority opinion, since humans are capable of achieving enlightenment either by their own power, as the Zen sect proposes, or through the merciful power of Amida Buddha, as Issa's own Pure Land sect, Jōdoshinshū, teaches. Nevertheless, Issa may be humorously asserting in his enigmatic haiku the contrary notion that human existence is actually best summarized, despite what most Buddhists might think, as "just so-so."

A close reading of the haiku in relation to clues in Issa's journals and in the cultural context of his time indeed raises more questions than answers, and one suspects that Issa would be glad of this. His elliptical art of haiku invites readers to meditate and discover their own truths as they ponder omissions and ambiguities that, one suspects (given his mastery of language), have been intentionally crafted. Of course, whether human existence is "remarkable" or just "so-so" ultimately depends on each reader's personal judgement. However, if we would like to attempt to figure out Issa's own answer to this question, and thus gain insight into a great artist's vision of the cosmos and the human role in it, we will need to examine and ponder hundreds of his haiku and related prose statements. This book will undertake exactly this examination, sifting carefully through Issa's writing to reconstruct as best we can the poet's panoramic view and philosophical understanding of human beings existing in the human society of early modern Japan: children and the elderly (our first and last chapters) and, in between, haiku portraits of farmers, priests, samurai, merchants, artisans, actors, singers, musicians, sumo wrestlers, geisha, prostitutes, beggars, outcastes, and thieves. What did "being born human" *really* mean to Japanese haiku poet, devout Buddhist, and famously comic, though sometimes darkly serious, social satirist Kobayashi Issa?

Let's find out.

Chapter 1. CHILDREN[6]

In First Month of 1797, 35 year-old Kobayashi Issa was in Matsuyama City, nearing the end of a long visit to the Japanese island of Shikoku. The leading poet of that city, 49 year-old Kurita Chodō, invited his younger counterpart to compose a 36-verse *kasen renku* with him. It was to be the sixth and last *kasen* that the two poets would write together. Since Chodō had made the *hokku* or starting verse for the previous *renku* earlier that month, it was now Issa's turn to lead off, which he did in the following way.

正月の子供に成て見たき哉 (1797; *IZ* 5.219)
shōgatsu no kodomo ni natte mitaki kana

becoming a child
on New Year's Day . . .
I wish!

New Year's Day, the first day of spring in the old Japanese calendar, was the most propitious day of the year. It evoked for people of Issa's era notions of youth, vernal regeneration, and buoyant optimism. It furthermore inspired religious devotion for the native gods whose shrines they visited, along with deep, patriotic feeling at the outset of a new imperial year. In fact, the day was also every citizen's birthday, since on New Year's Day everyone gained a year in age. The image of returning to a state of childhood serves as a powerful and fitting symbol for the rapture of such a day. While one might read Issa's *hokku* as mere wishful fantasy—to partake of the pleasures of the New Year's season, from tasty rice cakes to bright-colored kites, with the innocent, wide-eyed enthusiasm of a child—it can also *possibly* be read as a sincere and serious intention. In fact, a close reading of Issa's haiku about children and childlike awareness suggests that the notion of becoming a child not only pervades Issa's poetry, it helps to explain, perhaps more than any other single factor, his greatness as a poet. His approach to childhood is thus a logical starting point for our exploration of what being born human might have meant to him.

The idea of becoming a child isn't absurd if one considers the difference between child and adult to be more a difference in consciousness rather than in chronological age. Neuroscientists have attributed the transition from infant to adult consciousness to the development of a "Default-Mode Network" (DMN) in the human brain: crucial regions that receive more blood flow and consume more energy than other regions. Researcher Robin Carhart-Harris, in a 2014 study, equates these centers with Freud's concept of ego, a person's metacognitive sense of self. Whereas infants enjoy what Carhart-Harris calls pre-ego or "primary consciousness," this mode of awareness is gradually replaced by the DMN as a person matures. The DMN works to minimize surprise and uncertainty, and as a result much of one's sensory experience is screened out and raw emotions are suppressed, resulting in a state of consciousness that has contributed much to the survival of the human species . . . but at a high price. Carhart-Harris notes that the achievement of ego in the adult mind is at the cost of "emotional lability" as well as "our ability to think flexibly, and our ability to value nature" (Pollan 49).

A survey of Issa's poetry reveals that he envisioned his mission as a haiku poet to involve the valuing of nature and the universe with a flexible mind and nonjudgmental, primordial perception and feeling—in other words, with a state of consciousness that Carhart-Harris describes as primary. Sadly, most adults, due to their well-developed, rigid egos, rush past nature's treasures without truly attending to them, without *really* seeing, feeling, and coming to know them. Issa's *hokku* of 1797 might be read as a one-breath manifesto calling for a return to a different, earlier state of consciousness: to perceive and feel, once again, with childlike openness the world's infinite surprises.

Ironically perhaps, Issa most likely came to value the child's perspective through some quite grown-up reading of foundational texts of Buddhism and of the Taoism that infused itself into Buddhist tradition when that tradition passed through China, en route to Japan and other East Asian countries. In *Dao De Jing*, Laozi (Lao Tzu) praises unspoiled nature, such that a block of wood that no one has yet carved into a shape serves as a metaphor for the sage who remains in touch with his or her authentic way or *dao* (Chapter 15). Laozi also praises, fittingly, the spontaneous energy of babies.

> One possessing virtue may be compared to an infant.
> . . .
> Though weak in bones and soft in muscles,
> his hold is firm;
> Though ignorant of union, his instrument is turgid.
> This is supreme energy.
> Crying all day without turning hoarse,
> This is supreme harmony. (Tran. Li 121)

The baby (a male in Laozi's example) cries all day without getting hoarse because he simply follows his nature without struggling against it. His mind is not yet shackled with limitations imposed by the adult ego; neurologically, he enjoys what Carhart-Harris calls primary consciousness, and such consciousness, Laozi suggests, enables a life of more authentic virtue than that lived by so-called "educated" adults. Issa, well-read in the Chinese classics, was most probably familiar with the writings of Laozi, known as Rōshi in Japan. In any case, he certainly knew and followed Jōdoshinshū Pure Land Buddhism, whose founder Shinran teaches that innocent, pure-hearted trust—a virtue associated with children—represents the pinnacle of Buddhist devotion. Issa's decision to learn (more accurately, *un*learn) from children can thus be understood as a reasonable option within the wisdom tradition of Taoist-influenced Buddhism.

Jack Kerouac, a pioneer of English-language haiku, understood childlike consciousness to be essential in the process of composing such poetry.[7] In *Dharma Bums*, for example, Kerouac's first-person narrator observes, "Walking in this country you could understand the perfect gems of haikus the Oriental poets had written, never getting drunk in the mountains or anything but just going along as fresh as children writing down what they saw without literary devices or fanciness of expression" (59). Many poets have followed Kerouac's path of "going along as fresh as children" in their creation of haiku, stifling as much as possible grownup thoughts of literary fanciness. In fact, one might argue that the best haiku poets in our time, without exception, write in this way. A close examination of Issa's respect for, and emulation of, children not only helps to answer the question of what being human meant to the poet; it places into sharper focus the Japanese cultural and philosophical precedents for a crucial element in contemporary haiku.

In one of his poetic diaries, *Oraga haru* (1819), Issa writes glowingly about his infant daughter, Sato.

> I believe this child lives in a special state of grace, and enjoys divine protection from Buddha. For when the evening comes when once a year we hold a memorial service for the dead, and I have lit the candles on the family altar, and rung the bell for prayer, she crawls out swiftly, wherever she may be, and softly folds her tiny hands, like little bracken sprouts, and says her prayers in such a sweet, small voice—in such a lovely

way! For myself, I am old enough that my hair is touched with frost, and every year adds waves of wrinkles to my brow, yet so far I have not found grace with Buddha, and waste my days and months in meaningless activity. I am ashamed to think my child, who is only two years old, is closer to the truth than I. (*The Year of My Life* 94)

Though in his translation of this passage Nobuyuki Yuasa refers generically to Buddha, Sato's prayer is more specifically directed to Amida Buddha, "*Nanmu Nanmu*" being a baby's simplified and somewhat slurred version of the *nembutsu* prayer, "Namu Amida Butsu" ("All Praise to Amida Buddha!"). Issa's comment that he has not yet "found grace with Buddha" thus refers, in his original text, to the grace of Amida (*Issa Zenshū* 6.148). As a follower of Jōdoshinshū, the popular Pure Land Buddhist sect founded in the thirteenth century by Shinran, Issa believed it to be virtually impossible, in the present depraved age, for one to earn one's rebirth in Amida's Pure Land by meditation, asceticism, good works, or following Buddha's precepts. Such self-powered efforts (*jiriki* 自力) are doomed to fail in our corrupt time due to the tainting influence of self-interested calculations in the service of ego, in other words the Default-Mode Network described by neuroscientists. If enlightenment requires surrendering the fiction of the ego, any ego-powered method to reach it, Shinran reasoned, can't possibly work. For Shinran, the ideal candidate for rebirth in Amida Buddha's Pure Land and subsequent enlightenment is not a clever or educated person, but—as D. T. Suzuki points out in *Shin Buddhism* —a simple, innocently faithful believer who whole-heartedly trusts without question the "Other Power" (*tariki* 他力) of Amida Buddha. In Issa's religion (and/or philosophy, depending on how one conceives of Buddhism), a pure-hearted child is therefore closer to enlightenment than a self-interested, obsessively calculating adult—which is why Issa idealized not just children in his haiku but "innocent" animals as well.

立秋もしらぬ童が仏哉　(1814; *IZ* 1.430)
tatsu aki mo shiranu warabe ga hotoke kana

not knowing that
autumn's begun, a child
Buddha!

けさ秋としらぬ狗が仏哉　(1820; *IZ* 1.430)
kesa aki to shiranu enoko ga hotoke kana

not knowing that
autumn's begun, puppy
Buddha!

In these twin haiku Issa plays with the Japanese expression, "know-nothing Buddha" (*shiranu ga hotoke* しらぬが仏), which signifies, "Ignorance is bliss." In the context of Pure Land Buddhism, however, the cliché acquires an added layer of meaning. The puppy and the child are spiritually advanced not despite their ignorance of autumn's beginning but *because* of it. They revel innocently in the present moment without anxiety about autumn, loss, or the inevitable end of things. They are not Buddhists but Buddhas, and as such, Issa suggests, their way of being in the world is worth emulating.

Issa's own childhood, because of the death of his mother when he was just three and his father's subsequent marriage to an abusive stepmother, was marked by deep sorrow. His later experiences with children of his own, the first four of whom died young, was also famously painful. Nevertheless, a majority of his haiku about children are upbeat celebrations of their innocence, spontaneity, imaginations, and energy. A representative example is perhaps his most famous portrait of childhood, and suggests how an adult poet might return to a state of primary consciousness in order to become, in his heart and imagination at least, a child again.

雪とけて村一ぱいの子ども哉　(1814; *IZ* 1.95)
yuki tokete mura ippai no kodomo kana

snow melting
the village brimming over . . .
with children!

Kai Falkman cites this poem as an illustration of "the mechanism of surprise in haiku" (38). The first phrase provides an image of melting snow, and the second suggests a possible dire consequence: the village is "full" (*ippai*). Is it perhaps flooded? The third phrase, however, ends the haiku with a twist and a surprise: the village *is* flooded . . . *with children!* After setting up the reader with images of snow melting and a village brimming over, Issa delivers his punch line. The children of the village have been cooped up in their homes during the long, cold winter. Now, as snow finally liquefies under the springtime sun, they burst outside from their confinement, "flooding" the village: shouting, playing, laughing. Issa opens his senses, heart, and mind to the depths of the moment. The resulting poem is not a labored-upon product of calculation, not dressed up in what Kerouac described as "fanciness." Instead, it evokes, simply and spontaneously, a childlike state of freedom and joy.

Three years later, in 1817, Issa conjures a similar scene of youthful spontaneity and energy.

大根で叩きあふたる子ども哉　(1817; *IZ* 1.726)
daikon de tataki autaru kodomo kana

a battle royal
with radishes . . .
children

Little samurai wield large radishes (*daikon* 大根) in their rollicking battle. Not pictured in the poem, but implied, are the children's parents: grownup farmers stooping in a field, pulling up radishes. The children's lively creative play contrasts with the dull drudgery of the adults. The reader needn't guess where Issa's deepest sympathies lie. Once again, his haiku style of uncontrived simplicity perfectly matches his subject matter and intimates that, in terms of consciousness, the poet is tapping into that of his own inner child, and inviting his readers to do the same.

In several of his haiku portraits of children, Issa suggests that a child's perspective is instructive.

迷子のしっかり掴むさくら哉 (1814; *IZ* 1.229)
mayoigo no shikkari tsukamu sakura kana

the lost child
clutches them tightly . . .
cherry blossoms[8]

The poem evokes deep and conflicting emotions. At first, the reader may feel pity for the lost child, but upon further reflection, pity may give way to an "Aha!" moment. The child isn't crying for his (or her) mother. Instead, he clings to a branch of cherry blossoms. Perhaps he isn't even worried about being lost; the flowers are so lovely, such a prize to hold! When one views the haiku in this light, the child's attitude reveals a lesson for Issa's adult readers. One shouldn't fret about the future but instead should pay attention to the exquisite beauty of this world, here and now: relax the Default Mode Network's grip for a moment and appreciate nature as all of us once did when we were small.

Two haiku about a child tied to a tree, which in Issa's day was a form of "time out" punishment for naughtiness, similarly focus on innocent openness to nature.

わんぱくや縛れながらよぶ蛍 (1816; *IZ* 1.360)
wanpaku ya shibarare nagara yobu hotaru

naughty child
though tethered calling
fireflies

わんぱくや縛れながら夕涼 (1816; *IZ* 1.323)
wanpaku ya shibare nagara yūsuzumi

naughty child
though tethered enjoys
evening's cool

In both poems, the child is physically tied but free in his heart and mind. Adult readers of Issa, in his time and today, were and are tied invisibly to jobs and to all the daily worry that responsibility imposes, hence unable or too busy to call out to fireflies or revel in the pleasurable feeling of cool air on a summer evening. The naughty child, therefore, has something important to teach adults. Issa's lost and tethered children appear closer to nature than the majority of their elders, just as Issa believed his baby daughter Sato was closer than he to Amida Buddha and enlightenment. In the poet's mind, the advantage that children enjoy over most adults is their openness: to nature and to Buddha's grace. Following their example, Issa suggests, represents a huge step not only toward a deeper appreciation of nature but also toward rebirth in the Pure Land and enlightenment.

Childlike openness is also helpful, Issa suggests, when making art.

子宝が棒を引ても吉書哉 (1821; *IZ* 1.42)
ko-dakara ga bō wo hiite mo kissho kana

the treasured child
writes with a cane . . .
year's first calligraphy

Since Issa lived in Shinano Province's high elevation Snow Country, the child in the scene is most likely using the cane to create in snow or slush the calligraphy traditionally drawn on the second day of New Year's season, usually an auspicious poetic verse or, in the case of a very young child, a simple but meaningful symbol of hiragana. In one of his diaries Issa writes two possible opening phrases for this haiku, side by side: "treasured child" (*ko-dakara*) and "little priest" (*ko bōzu*), the latter an expression that can be taken literally to mean a young Buddhist acolyte or figuratively to mean any little boy (*IZ* 4.271). Though it has a New Year's seasonal reference, Issa composed the haiku in Ninth Month of 1821; his third child, Ishitarō, was then almost a year old. Though Ishitarō would have been too small to write with a cane, the poem might represent an imagining of the future of the poet's own "treasured child," who later that winter, sadly, would die of suffocation, bundled too tightly on his mother's back. In Issa's Japanese text the particle *mo* ("also") underscores the notion that the clever child has invented an alternative approach to New Year's calligraphy writing: that this action can be performed not only with a brush but "also" with a cane. Hence, the poem places emphasis on the child's creativity: thinking outside the box to scratch out a huge word in what we can imagine to be as much a moment of play as one of artistic expression. Having fun and making art are one in the same thing, at least in this moment, for this child.

The image of someone using a cane for New Year's writing appeared in an earlier verse, written a year before Ishitarō's birth.

ついついと棒を引ても吉書哉 (1819; *IZ* 1.42)
tsui-tsui to bō wo hiite mo kissho kana

swish, swish
writing with my cane ...
year's first calligraphy

For my translation I decided to picture the poet actively involved in the scene: the kind of self-satirizing self-portrait so common in Issa's poetry. However, his language also permits us to imagine "his cane" or "her cane" in use. In this cane-writing poem of 1819 Issa might actually have had a child in mind, in fact, since in his journal it immediately follows a haiku about a child making New Year's calligraphy, though presumably in a traditional manner.[9]

書賃のみかんみいみい吉書哉 (1819; *IZ* 1.41)
kakichin no mikan mii mii kissho kana

looking, looking
at the mandarin orange ...
year's first calligraphy

The orange is described as the "writer's fee" (*kakichin* 書賃), and since the writer's longing gaze is expressed in children's idiom (*mii mii* みいみい), we know the subject to be a child. In this funny, tender, and endearing portrait Issa captures the single-mindedness of a child who thinks so fixedly about the promised treat that he or she keeps looking up at it, as if to make sure that it's still there. Unlike the haiku about cane-writing, this one presents New Year's calligraphy not as fun or spontaneous but rather as an adult-supervised chore with an adult-provided reward. Though humorous, Issa's poem honors and focuses our attention on the child's purity of mind. The mandarin orange has become his or her whole universe. Issa invites adult readers to recall the amazing allure of a sweet fruit or rice cake (or, in the West, a fresh-baked cookie or ice cream cone) as it felt before the developing ego deadened the freshness of perception and the purity of desire.

A third haiku about calligraphy suggests that Picasso was correct when he described all children as artists, plunging fearlessly into their raw materials. When cooking, as much flour ends up on hands and faces as in the mixing bowl; when making calligraphy, as much ink ends up on hands and faces as on the rice paper.

あついとてつらで手習した子かな (1819; *IZ* 1.250)
atsui tote tsura de tenari shita ko kana

ink-stained hands
sweaty face . . .
the child's calligraphy!

The editors of *Issa zenshū* explain: "A sweaty face has been rubbed with ink-covered hands" (6.142). The result is the comic image of a child's face—perhaps that of Issa's own daughter Sato—smeared with ink. The image testifies to a child's unhesitant, non-censoring immersion in the creative process: a happy, messy, visual parable for Issa's readers to contemplate and, ideally, to emulate.

There are others, but for the purpose of the present chapter one more example of a haiku about a child's calligraphy deserves our consideration.

小坊主や筆を加へて梅の花 (1822; IZ 1.204)
ko bōzu ya fude wo kuwaete ume no hana

the little boy's writing brush
in his mouth . . .
plum blossoms

Again Issa describes a boy as a "little priest," and, again, the child's focus of attention fixes firmly upon something other than the calligraphy that he should be doing—whether for New Year's good luck or, perhaps, as schoolwork, since many Edo-period children received formal instruction at temple schools, memorizing and writing Chinese-based *kanji*. Instead of writing with it, however, the little boy chews on his brush while gazing (through an open window or door, perhaps?) at a blooming plum tree. In this scene he is not immersed in the art of calligraphy but *is* immersed, none-the-less: focused fully on the blossoming plum, a sign of early spring which symbolically complements his youth and freshness of perspective. It fills the boy's daydream with a vision of nature's wonder in the present, precious moment.

The next example of a child's portrait by Issa is a personal favorite.

凧抱て直ぐにすやすや寝る子哉 (? ; *IZ* 1.47)[10]
tako daite sugu ni suya-suya neru ko kana

hugging his kite
soon he's sound asleep . . .
the child

Flying kites was a New Year's activity for boys in Issa's day. This particular boy has evidently spent all of his energy in the excitement of the day and now sleeps, hugging his beloved kite. The haiku paints a picture of pure, trusting love: the love of a child for a toy. Even in sleep, the child's guileless, trusting way of being in the world, in Issa's depiction, is instructive for adult readers.

A more famous haiku portrait of a child by Issa, extant in two versions, illustrates again a form of consciousness utterly attentive and alive to the here and now.

庭のてふ子が這へばとびはへばとぶ (?; *IZ* 1.175)
niwa no chō ko ga haeba tobi haeba tobu

garden butterfly—
the child crawls, it flies
crawls, it flies . . .

門の蝶子が這へばとびはへばとぶ (?; *IZ* 1.175)
kado no chō ko ga haeba tobi haeba tobu

butterfly at the gate—
the child crawls, it flies
crawls, it flies . . .

In these undated haiku the poet presents a little motion picture: a baby crawls through bright green grass toward a butterfly. When the baby nears it, the butterfly flits away, only to alight a little farther off. Undaunted, the baby crawls again toward the colorful, fascinating apparition which, again, flits away. Baby and butterfly thus play a stop-and-go game of Catch Me If You Can. Like the young calligraphers in previous examples who single-mindedly focused on mandarin oranges or plum blossoms, the baby crawling toward the butterfly fixes utterly upon the object of sensation and desire. Issa in this way offers readers yet another glimpse into the purity of experience enjoyed through a primal mode of consciousness that predates the development of the adult brain. The baby is completely open, completely devoted to the sensations of here and now.

When I presented the first version of the above haiku to university students taking my World Literature course, one of these young, perceptive readers detected allegory. Leslie Anderson theorized that,

> The child symbolizes the human position, and the butterfly symbolizes transformation or improvement. Issa ingeniously relays that it is a natural instinct for human beings to desire or seek greater dreams. Perhaps, in the eyes of Issa, such dreams may have included rebirth. Although the butterfly (dreams) may seem beyond reach, the child (humans) does not crawl forever. Eventually, he/she begins to walk, then grow and, ultimately, he/she is able to touch the butterfly (his/her dreams).

Ms. Anderson's belief that Issa is disguising a more general, symbolic truth in the scene seems reasonable. The baby might indeed stand for all of us; if so, the butterfly that the baby chases might stand for the myriad, colorful experiences in this marvelous universe, if only we open ourselves to them. Unlike Ms. Anderson, however, I don't choose to assign the achievement of the baby's dream to a distant future, after he or she has grown up and achieved "success" as adults define this word. The baby in the scene, I believe, lives out his or her dream here and now: open to the butterflies of this universe, fully present and fully appreciative. In my own choice of assigning symbolism to the haiku, Issa's message is not "Grow up and achieve!" but rather, "Remember and *see!*" He challenges readers to recall their own earliest perceptions—when they once crawled through lush, fragrant grass perhaps—and learn from the baby's example: to look up from the poem on the page and drink in the universe, here and now, that always has surrounded them, and still does.

Another student in the same World Literature class, Keishondra Sampson, interpreted the poem in terms of Pure Land Buddhism which, she noted, "teaches of reincarnation as everyone is moving toward becoming a Buddha and reaching Enlightenment. The child crawling and chasing the butterfly represents everyone chasing the hope of reaching Enlightenment." I believe Ms. Sampson is also essentially correct, though perhaps not exactly in the way her words were meant. If realization of the Pure Land is not thought of as a distant, future-life prospect but rather as a here-and-now awakening, then the baby in the haiku indeed might signify the Buddhist enlightenment toward which fervent believers aspire.

In a series of poems about children and the moon, Issa seems to be cracking a joke at their expense.

> 赤い月是は誰のじゃ子ども達 (1811; *IZ* 1.451)
> *akai tsuki kore wa tare no ja kodomodachi*
>
> which of you owns
> that red moon
> children?
>
> あの月をとってくれろと泣子哉 (1813; *IZ* 1.451)
> *ano tsuki wo totte kurero to naku ko kana*
>
> "Gimme that moon!"
> cries the crying
> child
>
> 名月を取ってくれろと泣く子哉 (1819; *IZ* 1.456)
> *meigetsu wo totte kurero to naku ko kana*
>
> "Gimme that harvest moon!"
> cries the crying
> child

The moon appears like a bright toy tantalizingly just out of reach; children, Issa suggests, badly want to possess it. In the first haiku of 1811 the poet's question seems predicated on the fanciful notion that the red moon is a ball and, as such, must be some child's property. He asks, playfully, to "which of you" (*tare no ja* 誰のじゃ) does it belong? Though superficially silly, on a deeper level the haiku draws attention to the fact that the resplendent moon belongs to no one and, therefore, to everyone—along with the stars, the sun, and all the glories of the universe. We are, therefore, the "children" that the poem actually addresses. The later two haiku of 1813 and 1819, in which a crying child reaches unsuccess-fully for the seemingly near moon-toy, also embed a serious idea within their humor. The child—alert and open to all the world's intriguing colors and inviting shapes—reaches covetously for the moon with a mind uncluttered by facts of astronomy or scale. Though disappointed, he or she reminds adults how it once felt to be wide open to a universe of infinite possibilities.[11]

Because they are open to things, children also possess an instinct for perceiving the inherent divinity of things—or so Issa implies in the next haiku.

梅がかや子供の声の穴かしこ (1813; *IZ* 1.197)[12]
ume ga ka ya kodomo no koe no anakashiko

plum blossom scent—
the voices of children
sound reverent

The normally boisterous children lower their voices reverently: *anakashiko* 穴かしこ.[13] By juxtaposing a tone of reverence and awe with the scent of plum blossoms, Issa implies what his contemporary on the other side of the Eurasian continent, William Wordsworth, refers to as the "natural piety" of children. Like his counterpart in England, Issa challenges readers to learn from the young. In Wordsworth's neo-Platonic conception, children are closer to the Over-Soul—that ocean from which all souls emerge—hence more likely to experience "intimations of Immortality" than are adults. For Issa, operating in a Taoist-Buddhist tradition, children are closer to enlightenment than adults because they have not yet constructed self-interested, endlessly calculating mental barriers against it.

Though Issa and Wordsworth could not have known each other's work, they arrived at similar conclusions regarding the irresistible pull of nature to children who have not yet succumbed to the fiction of their separation from it.

> 裸子が這ふけしの咲にけり (1812; *IZ* 1.392)
> *hadaka-go ga harabau keshi no saki ni keri*
>
> the naked child crawls—
> the blooming
> poppies

The child is immersed in nature, one with nature. Without the clothing that symbolizes separation from the natural state (the most famous example being the fig leaves that Adam and Eve donned as they left the Garden of Innocence), this naked child of early modern Japan mingles with and loses his "self" in poppies. *Be* that child (again), Issa whispers to the reader, to all of us.

Issa's journals are filled with haiku that reiterate the theme of valuing and emulating childlike consciousness. For the purpose of this chapter, one last example will suffice.

> しら露としらぬ子どもが仏かな (1822; *IZ* 1.483)
> *shiratsuyu to shiranu kodomo ga hotoke kana*
>
> the child unaware
> of the silver dewdrops
> a Buddha

As noted earlier, "Know-Nothing Buddha" (*shiranu ga hotoke*) is an idiom for "Ignorance is bliss." Once again, Issa slyly transforms and subverts the cliché, suggesting that the child is indeed a Buddha, not simply metaphorically ignorant—just as an American poet today is free to use the expression, "When pigs fly," to convey the image of pigs *actually* flying, not merely to signify an abstract "Never." The dewdrops in the haiku carry special meaning in the context of Buddhism, for they are a conventional symbol in Japanese literature for Gautama Buddha's understanding of transience as a root cause of suffering: everything in the universe and the universe itself, like dewdrops evaporating in the morning sun, must ultimately pass away. The lucky child is indeed both ignorant and blissful, for he or she is unaware of the temporary nature of the universe, just as the child in an earlier example was unaware of autumn's start and all that this season of endings implies. The innocence of a child (or a puppy) entails for Issa a state of consciousness perfectly conducive to enlightenment, an ancient idea traceable back to Laozi's *Dao De Jing*.

In 1797, at the beginning of his poetic career, Kobayashi Issa expressed in the starting verse of a *renku* the wish to become a child on New Year's Day. For the next thirty years, following a spiritually informed approach to haiku, he fulfilled his wish. Adults *can* become children if they try, and this, Issa suggests, is a good thing.

Chapter 2. FARMERS

Under the rule of the shogun, Japanese society was officially divided into a hierarchy containing four divisions, the so-called *shinōkōshō* (士農工商): samurai, peasant farmers, artisans, and merchants. It was a societal model based on Neo-Confucian moral philosophy, according to which a class's higher status theoretically derived from its higher value to society as a whole (Deal 112). Samurai occupied the highest position due to their physical and supposed moral authority. Farmers, who produced the crops—especially rice, upon which society depended—were ranked second in importance. Artisans who created less essential products followed farmers, and merchants, who through their investments created personal wealth but nothing more tangible, came last. Left outside of this social paradigm were priests (both Buddhist and Shinto), and other large officially unrecognized groups, including prostitutes, beggars, and the oppressed ethnic minority of outcastes, the Ainu. This book will not follow the shogunate's ordering of social classes. Instead of beginning with the top-ranked samurai, we will first consider Issa's poetic treatment of farmers, since this is the social class into which he was born. The following chapter will look at his treatment of priests in light of the fact that the poet personally aspired to reshape himself into a "Priest of Haikai Temple." The remaining chapters will deal with Issa's verbal portraits of samurai, artisans, merchants, entertainers, prostitutes, beggars, Ainu, and thieves. Finally, since we began this study with a look at children and childlike consciousness in Issa, the book will conclude with an analysis of his poetic depictions of old people.

Yatarō Kobayashi's father, Yagobei, was a farmer who lived in Kashiwabara village in mountainous Shinano Province, today known as Nagano Prefecture. Young Yatarō would have been expected to follow in his father's footsteps, raising buckwheat, rice, and other crops on the nearly two acres of family farmland (Ueda 5), but a different destiny unfolded for the boy. When tension between him and his stepmother became unbearable in 1777, fifteen year-old Yatarō left for Edo, from which he somehow emerged, a decade later, as a haiku poet with the interesting penname of Issa, "One Tea" (一茶). Because of his long exile from his home village and hence from the agricultural lifestyle that he otherwise would have followed, Issa's attitude toward farmers, expressed in haiku, is that of a sympathetic outsider. When he first entered Edo's gates as an adolescent, he was one of thousands of peasants from the provinces who annually swarmed into the shogun's city as migrant workers, derisively labeled by Edoites as *mukudori* 椋鳥 or "starlings."[14] However, when he left Edo as a young man on his first haiku-writing journey in 1791, he was a peasant no longer. Issa had managed to step outside of the social designation of his birth. Like Bashō before him, he now had more in common with the priestly class of Tokugawa society than with any other. Whereas a peasant boy named Yatarō left Kashiwabara in 1777, "Priest Issa of Haikai Temple" returned to it, for a brief visit home, in 1791. In 1813, when his inheritance dispute with his stepmother and half-brother was finally resolved, 51 year-old Issa once again came to live in the farmhouse of his childhood, playing the dual roles of farm owner and poet but devoting most of his energy (and restless travels) to the second role.

A haiku written during Issa's beginning years as a wandering poet-priest suggests a feeling of guilty alienation from his peasant past.

もたいなや昼寝して聞田うへ唄 (~ 1790s; *IZ* 1.326)
motaina ya hirune shite kiku taue uta

ashamed
napping, hearing
the rice-planting song

The poem opens with the word *motaina* もたいな: a compressed form of *mottai-nai*.[15] The word has a rich, complex, and still-evolving history in Japanese semantics, making it impossible to capture all of its nuances with a single English equivalent. Issa's feeling of shame, hearing others singing and laboring in the rice paddies while he naps, on one level involves a sense of unfortunate waste. On another level, Issa's sloth may represent a religious failure as well. The root word *mottai* signifies intrinsic dignity or, in a Shinto understanding of it, intrinsic sacredness: the presence of divine, in-dwelling spirit in things. *Mottai-nai* therefore constitutes the negation of this dignity and/or spirit. For Buddhists, it more specifically can refer to the misuse of a holy object or dharma teaching. And, in a secular context of social dynamics, the expression can convey "a sense of gratitude mixed with shame for receiving greater favor from a superior than is properly merited by one's station in life."[16] Issa's shame in this haiku might include religious shame but also definitely seems to involve a feeling of secular, social embarrassment. His otherwise pleasant afternoon nap has been ruined by a guilty feeling that he's wasting time and, more damningly, he has not pitched in to help with the collective fieldwork that, in childhood, he was trained and expected to do. His self-accusing exclamation of *motaina* not only suggests that he doesn't deserve to relax while others toil; it underscores his social isolation that has come about as a result of his breaking away from his peasant roots and peasant identity. As so often is the case with Issa, the resulting poem is superficially humorous (he laughs at his own indolence), while at the same time, deeper down, it hints of a disturbing truth. The wandering poet-priest who no longer adds his voice to the rice-planting chorus is all alone . . . useless, spiritually defiled, and ashamed.

Issa returns to this theme of severed social roots and guilt in later poems, such as the following.

> 畠打や寝聳て見る加賀の守 (1824; *IZ* 1.118)
> *hata uchi ya nesobette miru kaga no kami*
>
> farmers plowing—
> lying down I watch
> Lord Kaga pass

By this point in his life, the poet once again was living in the home of his childhood—though partitioned so that he stayed on one side while his stepmother, half-brother, and his half-brother's family stayed on the other. Issa was physically back in Shinano province but psychologically and socially still separated from it. Others plowed while he was free to lie down, watching the local daimyo—Maeda, Lord of Kaga—pass by on the major highway near his home, the Hokkuko Kaidō (北国街道). Following the shogun's dictum that every provincial daimyo needed to maintain a residence in Edo and, each year, travel there along with their families, samurai, and servants; the fabulously wealthy Lord of Kaga and his vast, moveable household slowly troops by while Issa, surprisingly, remains lying down. Peasants would be expected to kowtow at the roadside at such a time, so Issa's reclining position might imply a dangerous and subversive lack of respect—or, perhaps, he is watching the procession at a sufficiently safe distance, which would release him from the obligation to grovel. Either way, the haiku reflects the fact that Issa has broken away from his former social role and its related social obligations, thanks to his new identity as a poet-priest. He no longer grovels for the daimyo, at least in this haiku self-portrait. (The situation for the real-life Issa may have been quite different.) This failure to humble himself in his haiku may not represent a rejection of the daimyo's power or of Tokugawa period etiquette; Issa might simply be implying that, as a Buddhist artist, he has emancipated himself from the human game of power and subservience and has thus achieved an enlightened outsider's perspective. Therefore, if on some level he may feel ashamed of his new, more privileged social situation, he might also feel perversely proud of it.

In another haiku self-portrait, he describes himself as *mudana mi* (むだな身): worthless, useless, good for nothing.

むだな身も呼び出されけり田植酒　(1822; *IZ* 1.328)
mudana mi mo yobidasare keri taue sake

even worthless me
is invited . . .
rice-planting sake

Issa has not participated in the rice planting, but the generous farmers nevertheless call to him, inviting him to enjoy sake with them. For the peasants, the liquor consumed during a rest break or at the end of the day represents a reward for their hard labor; for Issa, it's a gift offered, he admits, in spite of his worthlessness. And yet, one might note that in this and in the two previously discussed poems, Issa is only worthless as a farmer. As a poet, he is arguably a great success, producing insightful and intriguing verses while others work in the fields. "Good-for-nothing" Issa has, therefore also, ironically, been hard at work even while lying down . . . making this very haiku.

In a few of his poems written after his return to Kashiwabara, the poet might be hinting that, at least in part, he is reclaiming his peasant identity.

菜も蒔いてかすんで暮らす小家哉　(1815; *IZ* 1.86)
na mo maite kasunde kurasu ko ie kana

planting vegetables
living in mist . . .
little house

菜も蒔いてかすんで暮らす小家哉　(? ; *IZ* 1.86)
kyō mo kyō mo kasunde kurasu ko ie kana

today too, today too
living in mist . . .
little house

The first haiku, written in Second Month of 1815, could refer to Issa's return to his village and marriage to Kiku the previous year, in Fourth Month. If so, the poem sketches an idyllic vision of a wanderer's return to agrarian life and its simple pleasures. Like the surviving characters at the conclusion of Voltaire's *Candide*, Issa could be presenting himself as someone who has withdrawn from society's noise and injustices to tend, simply, to his quiet little garden in the misty hills. However, this poem of 1815 and its undated revision might refer as well, in the third person, to someone other than the poet: a humble and contented farmer, a person that perhaps Issa *wishes* he could be. Whether or not these are portraits of Issa's own late-in-life return to work the soil, these haiku certainly convey a tender feeling for growing crops far from the bustle of cities, high in Shinano's cloud-wrapped mountains.

Some of Issa's poetic snapshots of agrarian labor express feelings of deep appreciation, sincere affection, and, at times, nationalistic pride.

君が代は女も畠打にけり　(1815; *IZ* 1.117)
kimi ga yo wa onna mo hatake uchi ni keri

Great Japan!
a woman, also
digs with a plow

The poem's first phrase, *kimi ga yo* 君が代, refers literally to the "emperor's reign." Though the shogun in Edo ruled Japan, the emperor in Kyoto remained a revered and beloved symbolic head of state. The phrase is the first line of a Heian period *waka* poem that later, in the twentieth century, would provide the lyrics for the country's national anthem. In Issa's time the words already oozed with patriotism. By exclaiming, "Emperor's reign!" he is not only celebrating the person of the emperor; he is wishing that his reign will last long and embody a period of prosperity for all of the Japanese people. "Great Japan!" is my attempt at a translation of this complex sentiment. Significantly, Issa's haiku highlights the fact that Japan's prosperity depends on its agriculture (mainly rice production) and the fact that agriculture depends on the nation's hard-working peasants. A woman "also" (*mo*) pitches in to plow a *hatake* 畠: a field, garden, paddy, or plot. The greatness of the entire nation—the divine emperor's greatness included—thus flows, Issa suggests, from humble, nameless peasants: men and women sweating under the sun and plowing the good earth.

In an undated haiku, quite similar in tone to the preceding, Issa expresses pride more specifically for the farmers of his home province of Shinano.

しなのぢや上の上にも田うえ唄　(? ; *IZ* 1.328)
shinano ji ya ue no ue ni mo taue uta

Shinano road—
higher and higher
the rice-planting songs

Even at high elevations, rice-planting songs ring out in the terraced fields. Issa slightly alters the image in another version:

しなのぢや山の上にも田植笠　(1821; *IZ* 1.328)
shinano ji ya yama no ue ni mo taue kasa

Shinano road—
atop the mountain, too
rice planters' umbrella-hats

The first poem celebrates a discovery: as one climbs the Shinano road, higher and higher, one still finds, incredibly, paddies of rice filled with singing peasants. The second poem goes a bit farther to claim that even at the very top of a mountain peasants are working in rice fields, their heads shaded by rustic umbrella-hats (*kasa* 笠). Though the poem might be humorous exaggeration, it might also be literally true. Either way, it celebrates the indomitable, creative spirit of the peasants of Shinano. Even high on mountainsides they have improbably carved out fields to grow rice, the life-blood of early modern Japan's economic system. The value of each plot of land in Issa's time was measured in *koku* (石): the volume of rice that it could annually produce (Nouet 29). For example, the family of Issa's local daimyo in Shinano—Maeda, Lord of Kaga—had holdings worth over one million *koku* (83). This daimyo's extravagant wealth required legions of ingenious, hard-working peasants making rice grow at higher and higher points in the Shinano clouds. Issa's sense of pride in their efforts is palpable in these poems.

In the next haiku he depicts another peasant woman (or girl) hard at work in a field.

負ふた子も拍子を泣や田植唄　(1825; *IZ* 1.328)
outa ko mo hyōshi wo naku ya taue uta

> the child on her back
> cries to the beat . . .
> rice-planting song

Like so many women then and now, the rice planter in the scene works two full-time jobs. As agricultural laborer, she slogs through a flooded rice paddy, bending low to replant bright green stalks of rice plants. As a mother—or, perhaps, big sister—she cares for the baby bundled on her back. Like all of the peasants in previous examples, she contributes directly to the prosperity of Japan and to the glory of its daimyos and emperor, not only by producing wealth in the form of rice, but by giving birth to (if we imagine her to be the mother) and nurturing (whether we imagine her as mother or sister) a member of the next generation, so necessary for the future survival of the nation. The baby on her back and the fertile field with its promise of an eventual harvest both symbolize a prosperous future. The infant's wailing comically follows the rhythm of, and thus unintentionally adds to, the rice-planting work song. As one learns to expect with Issa's humor, beneath its surface deeper implications are discoverable. The peasant baby, even with his or her first vocal sounds, joins in with the rice-planting song, thereby affirming a lifelong identity as a rice grower. And Mother or Sister sings too, despite the double burden of farm labor and child-rearing, thereby illustrating the resilience and strength of the Japanese female farmer. Issa's haiku is a glowing tribute to a single nameless, strong peasant . . . and millions like her.

One might speculate that Issa's childhood identity as a farmer inspired his evident feelings of connection with, and compassion for, farmers that he encountered later in life and sketched in myriad haiku portraits.

> 雨の日やひとりまじめに田を植る(~1790's; *IZ* 1.326)
> *ame no hi ya hitori majime ni ta wo ueru*

rainy day—
alone and diligent
planting rice

小田の水おとした人も淋しいか　(1806; *IZ* 1.513)
oda no mizu otoshita hito mo sabishii ka

that farmer
draining his rice field . . .
lonely too?

薮陰やたつた一人の田植唄　(1815; *IZ* 1.327)
yabu kage ya tatta hitori no taue uta

in the thicket shade
all alone . . .
rice-planting song

In the above examples, a reader might sense the poet's heart opening wide with human feeling—with what Japanese call *ninjō* (人情)—for these solitary farmers. They work alone, without praise and not expecting praise, while unbeknownst to them Issa notices and implicitly praises them by sketching them in his poetry. In the second haiku, peasant-born Issa emphasizes an existential similarity with the peasant in the scene, when he wonders aloud if he "too" (*mo*) might be lonely. Two strangers—a farmer draining his muddy field and the poet observing and recording this labor—are very much alike in that they find themselves, in this moment, alone in the world. The third haiku tugs even harder at the reader's heart strings, as the farmer working in a thicket's shadows chants the usually communal work song by himself. Adding to the pathos of these scenes, it's possible that the lone farmers in them are suffering the punishment of *mura hachibu* ("the village eight"). As Prasol explains, "In those days, the villagers united in their efforts to help members of the community on 10 specific occasions [. . .] If somebody was to be punished, the commune would prohibit anybody's involvement in eight of them, hence the term" (226). Working in his field alone, the farmer in these three poetic portraits may be suffering from public ostracism. Whether or not this is the case, Issa, an outsider himself, seems to feel a profound sense of identification with these lone farmers.

For this next haiku, the reader need not search between its lines to guess at the poet's emotion; Issa states it outright in a headnote in his journal that reads, "Feeling pity for a widow alone in the world." The poem follows.

おのが里仕廻ふてどこへ田植笠 (1819; *IZ* 1.327)
ono ga sato shimaute doko e taue-gasa

when your village is done
where next?
rice-planting umbrella-hat

Perhaps he chose to include his brief prose preface because it adds a poignant piece of information that he was unable to fit into the poem itself but that he felt was important information: that the migrant farm laborer in question is a widow. With her husband dead she is now "alone in the world," Issa notes. Her status has changed but not her need to make a living, so after planting rice in her own village's fields, she must now move on to do this work in other villages, other fields. She inspires in Issa a feeling of pity (*awaresa* 哀れさ), though "pity" is a perhaps slightly misleading translation in this context, since this word in English can imply a feeling of moral or social superiority—something that Issa never claims. A poet who sees eye-to-eye with frogs and sparrows never looks down on itinerant rice planters. He is, in fact, like them: one of the downtrodden citizens of downtrodden Shinano Province.

下々も下々下々の下国の涼しさよ (1813; *IZ* 1.254)
gege mo gege gege no gegoku no suzushisa yo

it's a down, down
downtrodden land . . .
but cool!

The highland poet-persona, "Beggar Issa," appreciates Shinano's cool summer breezes, but he also, he reminds us often, shares in, and suffers from, its poverty.

Issa understood and sympathized with the plight of farmers and migrant agricultural laborers who made possible the wealth of Japan, but he was not an Edo-period Marxist. In the winter of 1813, he witnessed and wrote about a local peasant revolt. The uprising occurred on the 13th day of Tenth Month. That year's rice crop had disastrously failed, causing the price of rice to skyrocket. Unable to afford the life-sustaining staple that they themselves had planted and harvested, the hungry and frustrated peasants rebelled. The day before this insurrection, Issa was visiting Zenkōji, a major temple town in Shinano, where he had participated in a linked verse party in honor of Bashō's death anniversary. He describes the next evening in *Shichiban nikki* ("Seventh Journal") in prose: "13th day, clear. That night, at Zenkōji, night thieves rose up, every hand holding spears, woodman's hatchets and the like, breaking into rich men's houses . . ." (*IZ* 5.130). The peasants with whom Issa identifies so closely in other poems suddenly have become "night thieves" (*yanusumi* 夜盗), and their spontaneous revolt, he suggests in the haiku that follows, is an act of pure evil, not at all an expression of legitimate demands.

とく暮よことしのやうな悪どしは (1813; *IZ* 1.615)
toku kure yo kotoshi no yōna akudoshi wa

>end quickly!
>this year, you've been
>an evil one

One can argue (as I have done, elsewhere[17]) that Issa's coloring of spear and hatchet-wielding farmers as agents of "evil" was simply a strategic, self-preserving rhetorical choice, given the contemporary power structure. To defend rebels would have been dangerous, even if scribbled in a haiku poet's private journal. An alternative reading of the text, however, leads to a quite different conclusion: that Issa was frightened by and profoundly disapproved the violence of the mob; he could find no more apt word in his sophisticated poet's vocabulary than "evil" to describe what he had witnessed.

In other haiku portraits of farmers scattered throughout Issa's journals, he doesn't characterize them as evil, but he certainly criticizes them. For example, in the following poem, written a year after the Zenkōji insurrection, he alludes pointedly to the stinginess of Japanese peasants.

>惜るる人の青田が一番ぞ (1814; *IZ* 1.278)
>*oshimaruru hito no aoda ga ichiban zo*

>the stingy farmer's rice field—
>the first
>to turn green

Five years later in *Oraga haru* (1819), he employs the expression "Hauling water to *my* rice field" (*gaden insui* 我田引水; *IZ* 6.157) as a trope for selfishness. Keeping this later statement in mind, the reader might surmise that the "stingy" farmer in the 1814 haiku has been stingy with his water, hoarding it for his own field and not allowing it to trickle down into his neighbor's. As a result, his plot of rice naturally has turned green first. The color symbolizes fertility, life, and hope—especially the hope for a good harvest and the prosperity that it promises—but the field also is a bright green eyesore: flagrant evidence of a farmer's selfishness for prospering at his neighbor's expense.

In addition to their famous selfishness, Issa well understood—and was quite willing to express this understanding in haiku—the jealousies, petty anger, and myriad grudges harbored by peasant folk.

田植歌どんな恨みも尽ぬべし (1815; *IZ* 1.327)
taue uta donna urami mo tsukinubeshi

rice-planting song—
let everyone's anger
be cured!

The poem expresses the hope that the unifying work song of planting time (actually *re*planting time) might replace endemic peasant rancor with a benevolent sense of common purpose. Whether or not this hope was ever actually fulfilled, the haiku acknowledges a problem in the rural community while hinting at a possible solution: that anger at neighbors might be cured by the collective effort of rice planting. Peasants thus might put aside their grudges and realize that they are all, truly, "in this together."

Despite their stereotypical selfishness and wrath—or perhaps *because* of these traits and his desire to correct them—Issa sometimes makes a point of depicting peasant farmers behaving quite generously.

畠打が近道教ゆ夕べ哉 (1793; *IZ* 1.116)
hata uchi ga chikamichi oshiyu yūbe kana

the plowman
shows me a shortcut . . .
evening

大根引大根で道を教へけり (1814; *IZ* 1.726)
daiko hiki daikon de michi wo oshie keri

with a just-yanked
radish
pointing the way

菜畠を通してくれる十夜哉 (1819; *IZ* 1.657)
na-batake wo tōshite kureru jūya kana

he lets me cross
his field . . .
night of winter prayers

畠打や通してくれる寺参 (1823; *IZ* 1.118)
hata uchi ya tōshite kureru tera mairi

the plowman lets me
cross his field . . .
temple pilgrimage

Many more examples could be cited, but these four make the point that from his early work onward, the helpfulness of farmers allowing shortcuts through their precious fields became a recurring theme for Issa. In the third and fourth examples of 1819 and 1823, he invites a religious interpretation of peasant generosity, situating it in a distinctly Buddhist context. In the third haiku, on a night of winter prayers—one of the so-called "Ten Nights" (*jūya* 十夜) of Tenth Month during which pious Pure Land Buddhists chanted the *nembutsu* prayer to Amida Buddha and celebrated the prospect of rebirth in the Western Paradise made possible by Amida's Other Power—the normally self-absorbed farmer becomes other-serving and compassionate, like Amida. The fourth haiku presents a similarly religiously infused scene, as Issa describes, and implicitly praises, a farmer who allows him (or some other pilgrim) to take a shortcut through his field to visit a temple.

In other haiku portraits Issa celebrates farmers' closeness to nature.

> 畠打やかざしにしたる梅の花 (1808; *IZ* 1.116)
> *hata uchi ya kazashi ni shitaru ume no hana*
>
> giving shade
> for the farmer's plowing . . .
> plum blossoms
>
> 畠打やざぶりと浴る山桜 (1814; *IZ* 1.117)
> *hata uchi ya zaburi to abiru yama-zakura*
>
> plowing the field
> in a shower of mountain
> cherry blossoms
>
> 野らの人の連に昼寝やかたつむり (1823; *IZ* 1.387)
> *nora no hito no tsure ni hirune ya katatsumuri*[18]
>
> taking a siesta
> with the farmer . . .
> a snail

Plum blossoms provide them shade; cherry blossoms shower them with their delicate, pale pink beauty; snails share their midday naps with them. The farmers in these poems live professionally and literally close to the earth, its soil, its creatures, and its cycle of seasons. They therefore naturally enjoy the benefits of their proximity to nature. They spend whole days in the presence of spring blossoms; they sleep alongside snails on lazy summer afternoons.

In other moments, however, farmers in Issa's haiku appear crassly indifferent to nature's splendor.

畠打や手洟をねぢる梅の花　(1811; *IZ* 1.116)
hata uchi ya tebana wo nejiru ume no hana

plowing the field
and wiping snot
on plum blossoms

畠打や足にてなぶる梅の花　(1818; *IZ* 1.117)
hata uchi ya ashi nite naburu ume no hana

plowing the field
crushed underfoot . . .
plum blossoms

Though, as we have seen, he at times seems to praise farmers' proximity to nature's blossoms and creatures, Issa can't resist, on other occasions, the satirical impulse to de-romanticize agrarian scenes with blunt and shocking realism. In the above two examples the Japanese peasant is too busy to appreciate the blossoms—except, perhaps, as a convenient facial tissue. As his plow slices forward, he ignores and destroys the lovely fallen flowers: an early sign of spring valuable, in this case, not as an object for esthetic contemplation but rather, pragmatically, as mulch. These poems may in fact suggest a different way to read the previously cited ones. Perhaps the plowman shaded by blossoming plum and showered by falling cherry blossoms is working too hard to enjoy or notice this surrounding beauty; perhaps the napping farmer is too exhausted from his labor to know or care that he has been joined by a snail. In fact, despite their surface similarity as fellow nappers, on a deeper level of interpretation might the carefree snail be silently mocking the care-worn man? Issa and, by extension, the reader is able to imagine and appreciate nature's beauty in these haiku scenes, but perhaps the farmers in them are slaving too long and too hard to do so.

Issa's journals are filled with images showing how difficult life was for the peasants of cold, snowy, rugged Shinano.

> 一鍬に雪迄返す山田哉 (1821; *IZ* 1.116)
> *hito kuwa ni yuki made kaesu yamada kana*
>
> the same hoe
> plows the snow too . . .
> mountain rice field
>
> 雪ともに引くり返す山田かな (1822; IZ 1.116)
> *yuki tomo ni hikurikaesu yamada kana*
>
> plowing as much snow
> as earth . . .
> mountain rice field
>
> 山人や畠打に出る二里三里 (1823; *IZ* 1.118)
> *yamaudo ya hata uchi ni deru ni ri san ri*
>
> mountain man—
> off to plow his field
> five, six miles away[19]

In these far from idyllic verses farming appears as a strenuous, frustrating business requiring strong bodies and determined minds. The no-nonsense farmers of Japan's mountainous heartland must do what it takes to eke out their survival in this world while, Issa suggests, longing for the next.

菜の畠打や談義を聞ながら (1823; *IZ* 1.117)
na no hata uchi ya dangi wo kiki nagara

plowing the field
listening to
the sermon

In an effort to bring Buddhism to the masses, Pure Land preachers taught the possibility of rebirth in a glorious Western Paradise, a teaching tailor-made for Japan's hardworking peasants. As a devout follower of the widely popular Jōdoshinshū sect, Issa might not be injecting sarcasm or a critique of religion into the above haiku, but then again he might. Physically and financially drained peasants labor on, buoyed up and fundamentally misled by a crossroads priest's promise of pie in the sky. However, if his tone in this haiku is not satirical, Issa could be celebrating a sincere, heartfelt hope for these downtrodden plowmen. If they truly attend to the sermon—if they trust utterly in the Other Power of Amida Buddha—they could indeed draw closer to achieving enlightenment.

Born a peasant, Kobayashi Yatarō deeply understood and, in his new poetic identity as Priest Issa, compassionately portrayed farmers in haiku. At times, as we have seen, his own presence is either felt or outright announced in these poems, projecting the persona of a sympathetic but often alienated outsider. Despite his admiration for hardworking peasants, especially those living in his home Province of Shinano, Issa at times lampoons their selfishness and capacity for holding grudges. More typically, however, his haiku portraits of farmers praise their determination and grit, while implying that all the wealth of Great Japan arises directly from their toil.

半分は汗の玉かよ稲の露 (1822; *IZ* 1.579)
hambun wa ase no tama ka yo ine no tsuyu

> is half of it
> human sweat?
> rice field dew

Two conclusions can be drawn from such a haiku. First, Issa understood that part of the meaning of being born human, if born a farmer, involved extreme personal sacrifice so that life-sustaining and nation-enabling rice might grow. And second, one learns that Kobayashi Yatarō, though he later became a priest of Haikai Temple, never, ever, forgot where he came from.

Chapter 3. PRIESTS

Priests in Issa's verse depictions are most often Buddhist priests, though occasionally clerics of the native Japanese religion of Shinto appear.

> 権禰宜が一人祭りや木下闇 (1825; *IZ* 1.421)
> *gonnegi ga hitori matsuri ya ko shita yami*
>
> the Shinto priest's
> festival for one . . .
> deep tree shade

"Priest Issa of Haikai Temple" self-identified as a Buddhist rather than Shinto member of early modern Japan's religious ranks. This is not to say that Priest Issa in any way rejected Shinto faith or its popular year-round rituals. Like most Japanese people, he bowed both to the ancient, immanent gods of Shinto and to the Buddhas.[20]

> 君が世や寺へも配る伊勢暦 (1793; *IZ* 1.680)
> *kimi ga yo ya tera e mo kubaru ise-goyomi*
>
> Great Japan!
> even for a Buddhist temple
> Ise Shrine's calendar

In the previous chapter we explored a haiku that also begins with the semantically packed, difficult-to-translate phrase, *kimi ga yo* ("emperor's reign"). In that case, Issa indicated that the prosperity of the emperor's reign depended on hard-working, rice-planting peasants. In the present case, the discovery of a copy of a Shinto calendar in an unnamed Buddhist temple similarly inspires patriotic rapture. Both spiritual ways of being in the world, Issa suggests, contribute to the emperor's reign and Japan's greatness—a glowing endorsement of his nation's religious syncretism.

Though readers can usually tell either by verbal or contextual clues whether a given priest is Buddhist or Shinto, there exists another, often more puzzling ambiguity in many of Issa's haiku about priests. Since he identified himself as a Buddhist priest of the mythical Haikai Temple, it is at times impossible to know for certain if the subject in a particular verse is a self-portrait or a third-person description of another priest.

けさ春と掃まねしたりひとり坊 (?; *IZ* 1.27)
kesa haru to haku mane shitari hitori-bō

spring's first dawn—
the priest pretending
to sweep

通し給へ蚊蠅の如き僧一人 (1792; *IZ* 1.367)
tōshi tamae ka hae no gotoki sō hitori

let him pass
like a mosquito, a fly . . .
solitary priest

The first poem shows a priest on New Year's morning going through the motions of sweeping, its comic tone leading one to suspect that the priest in question might be the famously untidy poet himself, in whose "trashy hut's" unswept corners spiders can rest easy. However, the reader is also free to imagine a different priest than Issa giving a temple's floor a perfunctory swipe of the broom. The priest in the second, quite early example also might or might not be Issa. French translator Jean Cholley chooses the former option, picturing Issa as the "solitary" priest attempting to pass through a barrier gate. The haiku, Cholley suspects, is a sly jab at the authority of the shogunate (234). While Cholley may be correct in identifying Issa's satirical intent, it is impossible to tell for certain that he is the priest in question.

In other haiku, such as the next example, Issa more plainly identifies himself as the priest in the scene.

我もけさ清僧の部也梅の花 (1798; *IZ* 1.191)
waga mo kesa seiso no bu nari ume no hana

this morning I'm one
of the pure-minded priests . . .
plum blossoms

The poem appears in an early text, *Saraba-gasa* ("Umbrella-hat's Farewell"); Issa also used it as the first verse of a *renku* written in Matsuyama that same year of 1798. In both instances he prefaces it with the headnote, "Here I greet the spring." The word "here"—more literally, "in this place" (*kono uchi ni* 此裡に)—refers to a particular mountain temple where he was staying at the time (*IZ* 5.221; 1.191). The "priest" here not only is Issa; he boldly describes himself as one who has joined the ranks of the "pure-minded" (*sei* 清). Is he making this claim with a tone of self-irony, or might he be expressing a sincere claim of his own pure-mindedness? The open petals of plum blossoms visually reinforce an idea of ethereal purity. An early spring bloom, they can suggest a notion of rebirth. Spiritually, then, Priest Issa might be announcing in this poem that he is sincerely, profoundly starting life anew.

He was not alone in successfully transforming himself from peasant to priest.

秋風や角力の果の道心坊 (1823; *IZ* 1.471)
akikaze ya sumō no hate no dōshinbō

autumn wind—
the former sumo wrestler
a begging priest

The sumo wrestler, whom we can imagine was once vigorous and popular, has now fallen in social status to become a *dōshinbō* 道心坊: a begging Buddhist priest (*IZ* 4.446). As the year draws near to its end, the wrestler's life also transitions toward old age, while a bitter, chilling wind whispers of death's coming. Many of Priest Issa's self-portraits are less bleak but nevertheless depressing, suggesting that his transition from farmer to monk has constituted a formidable challenge to which he has not always completely risen. In the following examples, he describes himself as "defiled" and "worldly."

汚坊花の表に立りけり (1810; *IZ* 1.211)
yogore-bō hana no omote ni tateri keri

a defiled priest—
before the cherry blossoms
he stands

花さくや桜所の俗坊主 (1811; *IZ* 1.211)
hana saku ya sakura tokoro no zoku bōzu

spring blossoms—
in the cherry grove
a worldly priest

In neither of these haiku does Issa use a first-person pronoun, yet readers familiar with his work will immediately suspect that he must be the inadequate priest in them. Earlier, we noted that he portrayed himself as a failure as a farmer: napping while others toiled in the fields. The priest in each of the present examples is, in parallel fashion, a failure at Buddhism. The notion that Issa may be poking fun at himself for being as much a failure as a priest as he was as a peasant-farmer is hard to resist. Though he has adopted the identity of a Buddhist priest, Issa (Issa-like) confesses that he is a poor one. Gautama Buddha taught that the way to enlightenment involves letting go of attachment to temporary phenomena, an attachment that is the source of suffering. Nevertheless, the priest in these poems appears "defiled" and "worldly" among cherry blossoms; perhaps he cannot manage to detach his heart and mind from the world's alluring beauty. If Issa is indeed this priest, perhaps his identity as a blossom-loving haiku poet is clashing fatally with his new priestly identity. Amid the blooming groves of springtime, his poet's self seems to emerge victorious, hence the labels of "defiled" and "worldly" for his priestly self.

In other poems Issa's critique of priests is almost savage, referring to them as "dirty" and "good-for-nothing." Again, there is a high probability that he is critiquing himself.

>赤づきん垢入道の呼れけり (1815; *IZ* 1.689)
>*aka zukin aka nyūdō no yobare keri*
>
>a dirty priest
>in a red skullcap
>he's called
>
>木のはしの法師に馴るる夜寒哉 (1818; *IZ* 1.437)
>*kinohashi no hōshi ni naruru yozamu kana*
>
>the good-for-nothing priest
>is used to it . . .
>a cold night

In the 1815 haiku the priest wearing a red skullcap is "dirty," a clever pun involving two meanings of *aka* as "red" (赤) and as "dirty" (垢). In a similar vein, the 1818 haiku describes a priest as, literally, an "animal worthless to capture" (*kinohashi* 木のはし).[21] Such a good-for-nothing creature *must* be Issa. To call another person worthless sounds cruel and mean-spirited, but to label oneself as such is the stuff of humorous confessional poetry that aligns perfectly with many similar self-critiques scattered throughout Issa's work. If this interpretation is correct and the poet is admitting his own inadequacy as a priest in these haiku, this would seem to be an admission of religious failure. However, because Issa followed the Jōdoshinshū sect, religious failure might be understood, paradoxically, as religious success. The founder of Jōdoshinshū, Shinran, insisted that the "Self Power" (*jiriki* 自力) of following Buddha's precepts comprises a useless path leading not to the Pure Land but instead to the cauldrons of hell: a faith-based as opposed to works-based doctrine.[22] Issa might therefore have believed that a "defiled," "worldly," "dirty," and "good-for-nothing" priest is closer to enlightenment than his more ostensibly pious peers who follow Buddha's precepts to the letter. The poet's revelation of his sinfulness and of his inability to overcome it by self-effort identifies him as one who might therefore be spiritually advanced, in a Jōdoshinshū understanding. If the priests in the above four haiku stand for Issa, he is shaming himself without real shame. "Defiled" Priest Issa has no reason for shame, if his admission of imperfection indicates that he has abandoned the illusion of self-powered Buddhism.

In other verbal portraits of priests Issa leaves absolutely no room for ambiguity; he plainly describes other people and not himself. In some of these cases he pokes fun at authority figures within the priestly community.

僧正が野糞遊ばす日傘哉 (1804; *IZ* 1.302)
sōjō ga no-guso asobasu higasa kana

the high priest
poops in the field . . .
parasol

Issa catches the high priest of a Buddhist temple literally with his pants down, not a very flattering portrait. However, by showing even an honored high priest pooping, Issa calls to mind life's plenitude, which includes not only sublime moments under moon and blossoms but also the universal mandate of bodily functions. This comic portrait, instead of disrespecting the high priest, might more accurately be understood to be humanizing him. However, because the priest does his business under a parasol, the reader might reasonably imagine a second person in the scene: a young acolyte, perhaps, holding the parasol and politely looking away. The implied presence of a lower-ranked parasol holder imbues the haiku with an added element of satire. The high priest ridiculously insists on the privilege of his social standing even in an undignified moment that reveals him to be just another of the world's animals. Although Issa describes the priest's action with the highly formal verb, *asobasu* 遊ばす, he ironically juxtaposes this formal language in the poem with the low, common expression, *no-guso* 野糞: "field shit." In this way, he slyly pops the bubble of the high priest's pretentiousness and his fixation upon his supposed superiority.

In the next two examples, haiku written in Fourth and Sixth Months of 1822, Issa again humanizes highly ranked religious figures by bringing them down to earth.

夜涼みや大僧正のおどけ口 (1822; *IZ* 1.325)
yo suzumi ya ōsōjō no odoke kuchi

evening cool—
the great high priest
tells jokes

老僧の草引むしる日傘かな (1822; *IZ* 1.303)
rōsō no kusa hiki-mushiru higarakasa kana

old priest—
even while plucking grass
a parasol holder

In the first poem a high priest enjoys the coolness of a summer evening with a group of others—perhaps fellow priests, perhaps laymen. Though loftily ranked, the priest in question comes down to earth with his "joking mouth" (*odoke kuchi* おどけ口). Humor, Issa implies, is a great social leveler—just as the previous example reminded us, biological functions can be. The second haiku, appearing in *Hachiban nikki* ("Eighth Journal") two months later, is an immediate rewrite of the previous poem in the journal, which describes the grass plucker as a "holy man" (*shōnin* 上人). Issa rewrote the haiku to begin with "old priest" (*rōsō* 老僧) instead. An elderly cleric performs the exemplary physical labor of patiently trimming the temple lawn using only his hands. The priest is most likely a high priest, his status indicated by the parasol held by a presumably lower-ranked holder. Although manual grass-trimming can be understood to be a spiritually humbling act, the old priest in the scene ironically and comically refuses to undertake it without the luxury of a sunshade held by an underling. His show of "humility" thus, in fact, reveals pride. Perhaps Issa changed the image from "holy man" to "old priest" to emphasize and satirize the grass trimmer's all-too human insistence on social status within the hierarchical community of temple priests.

A haiku in which two flies "make love" on a high priest's head is a wonderful construct of multiple juxtapositions: sacred and profane, lofty and lowly, serious and silly:

僧正の頭の上や蠅つるむ （1825; IZ 1.376)
sōjō no atama no ue ya hae tsurumu

on the high priest's
head . . .
flies making love

As in previous examples, Issa humorously pops the high priest's ego bubble. He might be the supreme authority in the temple, but above him (literally) are two flies—which is funny enough, but the fact that they are fornicating makes the poem hilarious. One can imagine the priest solemnly addressing his fellow priests or perhaps even his congregation with edifying words about Buddhism, while the flies copulating atop his bald pate physically communicate their own, more concrete message. The image suggests that the high priest probably shouldn't take himself or his words too seriously; nor should the others who are listening to him; nor should the readers of this haiku. Above the abstractions of human social rank and socially encoded human language, two flies communicate a deeper truth. Like them, human beings are creatures bound to inescapable impulses. Desire and attachment being inevitable, their only hope for enlightenment is to rely utterly upon Amida Buddha's Other Power.

Issa occasionally fixes his poetic gaze on rank-and-file representatives of Buddhist clergy.

長閑さや垣間を覗く山の僧　（? ; *IZ* 1.59)
nodokasa ya kakima wo nozoku yama no sō

> spring peace—
> a mountain monk peeks[23]
> through a fence

The haiku parodies a scene from the eleventh century *Tale of Genji* by Murasaki Shikibu. In Chapter 5 of that famous work Prince Genji peers through a fence, catching sight of ten-year old Murasaki, the little girl whom he later will attempt to mold into his perfect woman. The poem's date of composition is uncertain, making it impossible to tell whether Issa wrote it before or after a haiku of 1809 that spoofs the same scene from *Genji*; in that poem he substitutes a "lover cat" for the Shining Prince.[24] In this related haiku, a Buddhist monk is cast in the role of the famous spying prince. On one level, Issa is simply following his regular practice of lampooning institutions and authority figures; the supposedly detached and otherworldly monk steps into the lurid and unsettling role of a Peeping Tom: Prince Genji peeking at a girl. Deeper however, the poem reminds us, yet again, that people are only people. A mountain monk, too, can peek through a fence, can desire, can sin—*will* desire, *will* sin—for he is a human being.

A haiku showing a monk's face being splashed with slush, requires some explanation.

雪汁のかゝる地びたに和尚顔 (1804; *IZ* 1.94)
yuki-jiru no kakaru jibita ni oshōgao

> splashed with slush
> close to the ground . . .
> a monk's face

Issa introduces the poem in his journal *Bunka kuchō* with a prose introduction, in which he writes that he saw a monk chained to a pillory for the crime of seducing a woman of his temple's congregation (*IZ* 2.261). Passersby walking through the slush accidentally, or perhaps on purpose, are splashing his face. Unlike the monk of the previous example, who may have harbored sexual thoughts while peering, Genji-like, through a fence; the monk in this more serious verse has followed his urges and now is suffering dreadfully. If Issa's program is to disclose the humanity of priests beneath their saffron robes, this vision of a helpless, convicted monk—his face smeared with cold, filthy slush—may be the most powerful and effective example of all. The monk gave in to his human lust and now, stoically, must bear his shame and suffering . . . like a man.

A haiku about a priest who loses a lottery strikes a more comic tone.

負くじの僧がはなさぬ湯婆哉 (1822; *IZ* 1.703)
make kuji no sō ga hanasanu tanpo kana

the priest who lost
the lottery won't give it up . . .
hot water bottle

The prize for the lottery winner evidently was the use of a *tanpo*, a hot water bottle that keeps one's feet toasty-warm under the quilts on cold winter nights. The temple in question seems to have only one such convenience, so the monks nightly draw lots to enjoy its comfort. One particular monk, though, clings to the coveted foot-warmer, refusing to surrender it to that night's winner. The haiku doesn't reveal, nor does it need to reveal, the ultimate outcome of this clash of wills in a temple, but simply by depicting it Issa underscores the ego-centeredness and imperfection—hence the humanity—of Buddhist priests.

Not all of Issa's haiku portraits of priests expose their failings. At times he presents them as spiritual leaders and worthy exemplars. For example, in some poems about priests interacting with animals, the former exhibit compassion for, and identification with, their fellow travelers to enlightenment.

> つつがなき鳥の巣祝へあみだ坊 (1804; *IZ* 1.125)
> *tsutsu ga naki tori no suiwae amida-bō*
>
> pray good health
> for the nesting bird!
> Amida's priest
>
> 卯の花に蛙葬る法師哉 (1804; *IZ* 1.422)
> *u no hana ni kawazu hōmuru hōshi kana*
>
> in deutzia blossoms
> the priest buries
> the frog

The first haiku appears in *Bunka kuchō*, a Second Month entry. The "priest of Amida Buddha" (*amida-bō* あみだ坊) might of course be Issa, but regardless of his precise identity, the poem urges (grammatically, commands) this priest to pray for a nesting bird's good health. The implication is that the bird deserves as much concern and prayers as pregnant human mothers. Amida's priest is the ideal person to recite such a prayer, since Pure Land Buddhism accepted the notion that all creatures are capable of rebirth in the Western Paradise and subsequent enlightenment. The second haiku, composed later that same year in Fifth Month, captures the tender and compassionate moment in which a priest buries a frog, a ritualistic act that calls to mind, again, the Pure Land Buddhist belief in an essential sameness among and connection between living beings.

In a haiku of 1820, a buck that has shed his antlers after rutting season playfully butts his head against a mountain monk's belly.

おとし角腹にさしけり山法師 (1820; *IZ* 1. 125)
otoshi-zuno hara nisashi keri yama-bōshi

the buck who shed his antlers
pokes his belly . . .
mountain priest

Issa wrote other haiku linking bucks without antlers with Buddhist monks, suggesting that antler-shedding is a deer's equivalent of head-shaving and thus beginning life anew as a priest.[25] The antler-less bucks in those haiku and in this one appear as fellow travelers whose season of sexual aggression and passion has passed. They have surrendered their weapons and are now ready for the next step toward spiritual advancement. In this warm and happy haiku, the buck and the man are peers on the road to the Pure Land; one butts the belly of the other, his equal and his chum.

In the next two examples, both written in 1804 on the 28th day of Eleventh Month, Issa portrays the religious fervor of certain Pure Land priests.

鉢敲今のが山の凹み哉 (1804; *IZ* 1.662)
hachi tataki ima no ga yama no kubomi kana

a monk beats his bowl—
by now a dent
in the mountain!

西山はもう鶯かはち敲 (1804; *IZ* 1.662)
nishi yama wa mō uguisu ka hachi tataki

in western mountains
a nightingale already?
a monk beats his bowl

Beginning on the 13th day of Eleventh Month and continuing for forty-eight days thereafter, priests would go on pilgrimage, reciting the *nembutsu* prayer and singing religious songs. Since they had to beg for food along the way, they announced their presence and need by banging loudly on wooden bowls. The *nembutsu* prayer, "Namu Amida Butsu" ("All praise to Amida Buddha!"), celebrates Amida's "Original Vow" (*hongan* 本願) to enable those who rely on his power to be reborn in the Pure Land, located somewhere in the mythic west. The "western mountains" (*nishi yama* 西山) in the second poem thus calls to mind Amida's way to enlightenment. The nightingale, whose song apparently has gushed much sooner than expected, hints of Pure Land perfection, perceivable in these western mountains so near (symbolically) to Paradise. The other haiku written on that day is a fun example of poetic exaggeration, somewhat reminiscent of Bashō's famous verse about the ear-piercing song of cicadas permeating solid rock.[26] A monk has beaten his bowl so persistently, Issa jokes, that by now he must have surely dented the mountain. The poem on one level may be perceived as a mere complaint about the noise that's possibly keeping Issa awake. However, the monk's energetic banging also signals, upon deeper reflection, his religious dedication. In both of these poems of priests banging on their begging bowls, Issa presents memorable images of Pure Land Buddhist practice and devotion.

In other haiku sketches of Buddhist priests, Issa emphasizes a profound and instructive connection to nature.

野談義や大なロへ雉の声 (1816; *IZ* 1.148)
no dangi ya ōkina kuchi e kiji no koe

sermon in the field—
the priest's wide-open mouth
a pheasant's voice

The pheasant's cry literally emanates *toward* an open mouth, presumably that of an itinerant preacher. Just as the priest's mouth opens, however, instead of his voice a pheasant's is heard—as if the bird is the one doing the preaching. The poem is yet another example of Issa's favorite rhetorical techniques of bait-and-switch humor.[27] Beneath this humor, as often is the case with Issa, deeper implications lurk. The pheasant's cry perhaps *is* a Pure Land sermon, and the pheasant, though unaware of this fact, perhaps *is* a priest. Issa's poem could be suggesting that both "priests"—human and bird—are proclaiming in their respective ways a shared truth about Amida Buddha's vow to make rebirth in the Pure Land and Amida Buddha's enlightenment a concrete possibility for all species.

In another haiku of 1816, also written in that same Third Month, light shimmers on cherry blossoms while a Pure Land priest chants the *nembutsu*.[28]

> 起臥も桜明りや念仏坊 (1816; *IZ* 1.230)
> *okifushi mo sakura akari ya nebutsu-bō*

> going about
> in cherry blossom light . . .
> Pure Land priest

The *nembutsu*, as mentioned before, praises the Other Power of Amida Buddha that enables rebirth in the Western Paradise where enlightenment might be attained by all. The ethereal light of the sun reflecting off cherry blossoms bathes a praying monk, giving him a saintly glow. Like the nightingale in an earlier example that warbled while a monk beat his bowl in the western mountains, the iridescent spring blossoms in this haiku hint of Pure Land perfection here and now, in this world. In this case, the flower-illumined priest seems to embody this perfection, this hope.

We have looked at some haiku in which Issa reflects on the imperfection of priests (himself included) and at other haiku that implicitly praise the compassion and sincere, exemplary faith of priests. In other poems that fit neither of these categories, he offers slice-of-life images of priests hard at work.

山住や僧都が打もさよ砧 (1815; *IZ* 1.515)
yamazuma ya sōto ga utsu mo sayo-ginuta

life in the mountains—
even priests
pound cloth at night

雨降や苔の衣を打夜とて (1814; *IZ* 1.515)
ame furu ya koke no koromo wo utsu yo tote

rain falls—
a night for pounding
the monk's rough clothes

しがらきや大僧正も茶つみ唄 (1814; *IZ* 1.113)
shigaraki ya ōsōjō mo cha tsumi uta

Shigaraki—
even the high priest sings
a tea-picking song

老僧が炭の打ったを手がら哉 (1822; *IZ* 1.706)
rōsō ga sumi no otta wo tegara kana

for the old priest
breaking charcoal . . .
a feat

In Japan and Korea, wooden mallets were traditionally used to pound fabric and bedding. The fabric was laid over a flat stone, covered with paper, and pounded, making a distinctive—and in Issa's time, nostalgic—sound. The monks in the first two examples perform this labor at night, the *clonk-clonking* of their work echoing in the darkness. The phrase in the first haiku, "even priests pound," subtly underscores the fact that despite their spiritual aspirations, Buddhist priests are just like everybody else—that is, everybody else in the working class, for they must pound their clothes. In the second haiku the mallet beat of a monk (or several monks) accompanies the pattering of rain, making a sort of lonely duet in the night. In the third example, which takes place in the temple town and ceramics center of Shiragaki, the word "even" (*mo*) again is significant, drawing the reader's attention to the fact that even a high priest works with his brother monks, picking tea leaves. The fourth example suggests that the hard work for priests in Tokugawa Japan continued even later into life, as an elderly cleric, despite his feebleness, manages to break up some charcoal with which to heat the temple on a cold winter day or night. These poems—and many more that could be cited—depict Buddhist priests as down-to-earth, diligent workers, reminiscent of Issa's countless similar portraits of peasant farmers.

The similarity is significant. In Issa's poetic vision priests are as essential as peasants to the social fabric of Japan. In fact, they might even constitute, in his opinion, its gravitational center.

君が代や鳥も経よむはちたたき (1813; *IZ* 1.662)
kimi ga yo ya tori mo kyō yomu hachi tataki

Great Japan!
a bird recites a sutra
a monk beats a bowl

As in previous examples, the bowl-beating monk belongs to one of the Pure Land sects, reciting the *nembutsu* while on a winter pilgrimage. The haiku's opening, *kimi ga yo* 君が代, is the same patriotic invocation of the emperor's reign and prosperity with which, we have seen, Issa begins a few of his praise-poems celebrating Japan's hard-working farmers. In this particular verse he imagines that even a bird of Japan is devout, for his song is a sutra: a Buddhist holy text.[29] At the core of the emperor's greatness, hence of Japan's, lies its Buddhism, Issa implies: a faith so pervasive that even the birds in the trees are warbling its texts and truths. The *nembutsu* prayer that the monk recites, we have noted, proclaims Amida Buddha's vow to pave a way to a universal enlightenment that will benefit birds as well as people. Despite the imperfections of Japan's priests, including those of Priest Issa himself (or perhaps *because* of these imperfections, in light of Shinran's rejection of self-powered enlightenment); Japan appears as a great nation that has become great in large part due to the deep religious faith of its people. Japan's Buddhist priests have made this faith possible by preaching, praying, and beating their bowls. They thus lead the way to Amida's Western Paradise, and Priest Issa is among them.

Chapter 4. SAMURAI

During Japan's Tokugawa or Edo period, 1603 to 1868, the shogun in Edo exercised full political power, reducing the role of Kyoto's emperor to that of symbolic head of state. Presiding over an inventive hierarchy of 300 domain lords (daimyo), the shogun exercised centralized, national power, while the various ranks of daimyo ruled in their respective regions. The samurai class consisted of armed clan members who enforced the authority of shogun and daimyo at the local level. In a period of Japanese isolationism and relative domestic peace (with the exception of occasional peasant revolts, like the one that Issa witnessed in 1813, discussed in Chapter 2), samurai in the employ of the government functioned as feared and, often, hated police. Unemployed samurai, the so-called *rōnin* 浪人 or "master-less" warriors, instilled even greater fear and loathing in the hearts and minds of a populace that, by law, could not bear arms other than short swords (*wakizashi*), and then only while traveling (Cunningham 22). In a haiku about holly, a plant believed to bring good luck at the end of the year, Issa pointedly places *rōnin* and demons in the same category.

鬼よけの浪人よけのさし柊　(1819; *IZ* 1.681)
oni yoke no rōnin yoke no sashihiragi[30]

protection from demons
and wild samurai . . .
lucky holly

"Wild samurai" is my translation of *rōnin*: men who, Issa declares, were dangerous enough for commoners to require magical protection from them. Samurai, even those who had masters, were simply not to be reasoned with. According to Yamamoto Tsunetomo's early eighteenth century guidebook, "The Way of the Samurai," a samurai's greatness depended not on his "common sense" but rather on his ability to behave in an "insane and desperate" fashion: to be, literally, "crazy to die" (45; 171). The *rōnin* who served no lord or social purpose were especially crazy in Yamamoto's sense, thereby becoming "the terror of the middle class," prompting authorities to ultimately ban them from Edo's city limits (Nouet 85). Later in the nineteenth century, when Commodore Perry arrived in Edo's harbor (1853), a belligerent faction of *rōnin* argued (unsuccessfully) to make war rather than to come to terms with the United States, thus living up to their reputation for problem-solving through quick and irrational violence (174). Issa's little joke at their expense in 1819, equating them with demons, has deep historical resonance.

Issa's notebooks are filled with poetic sketches of Tokugawa period men of arms, some reviled and some respected. One of his most interesting and memorable of these haiku refers to warriors (or, possibly, to a single warrior) no longer present in the scene.

兵が足の跡ありけしの花 (1803; *IZ* 1.392)
tsuwamono ga ashi no ato ari keshi no hana

in the footprints
of warriors . . .
poppies

Where a "warrior" or "warriors" (*tsuwamono* 兵) once stepped, poppies now bloom—a powerful and complex juxtaposition of absence versus presence, humanity versus nature, war versus peace, death versus life. Left to the reader's imagination is whether or not the warrior or warriors recently trampled the flowers, or if the flowers happen to be blooming in a place where a battle once took place. If we picture the passing through of the warrior(s) as a recent event, the haiku might be interpreted as a satirical critique of samurai for so nonchalantly crushing the defenseless flowers, which could symbolically represent peasants. However, if we choose to picture the scene as a description of a long-ago battlefield, a more optimistic message emerges: an age of peace (the Tokugawa era) has replaced one of violence (the Heian period), Tokugawa poppies flourishing where Heian warriors once fought.

Both interpretations are possible and, perhaps, desirable. Much of the beauty and power of haiku derive from the poet's refusal to become overly specific, thus leaving plenty of space in which the reader's imagination can play. However, some textual evidence exists to favor the second interpretation of the scene. In the first place, Issa uses the old Heian term for warrior, *tsuwamono*, not the more contemporary "samurai." Secondly and even more tellingly, the haiku strongly echoes a famous verse written by Issa's predecessor and poetic role model, Matsuo Bashō.

夏草や兵共が夢の跡 (1689; Matsuo Bashō 1.271)
natsukusa ya tsuwamono domo ga yume no ato

summer grasses—
what's left
of warriors' dreams

In both haiku—Bashō's and Issa's—the old term for warrior, *tsuwamono*, appears in connection with plant life along with the phrase, *no ato* の跡: "aftermath." In Bashō's seventeenth-century haiku—found in his travel journal, *Oku no hosomichi* ("Narrow Road to the Interior")—the "aftermath" of the warriors' dreams turns out to be summer grasses. In Issa's nineteenth-century (possible) parody, the "aftermath" of warriors passing through is a field of poppies. In both poems plants thrive peacefully where warriors once clashed.

In an informative essay, Paul Rouzer explains that Bashō's haiku alludes to an even earlier poem: an eighth-century Chinese verse by Du Fu that begins with the couplet, "The state is smashed; rivers and hills remain./ The city turns to spring; grass and trees grow thick." Rouzer notes that Du Fu's verse, in turn, echoes a long tradition of previous works wherein poets of old China depicted the sites of ruined cities and reflected on their fall to oblivion. Du Fu, Rouzer notes, "was trapped by rebel forces in the Tang dynasty capital of Chang'an," so his verse about a smashed state is more of a prophetic vision than an actual contemplation of past violence. When Bashō visited the ruined fortress of a twelfth-century warlord, Fujiwara no Hidehira, he alluded to Du Fu's lines to evoke a feeling of lost lives, lost dreams, and a lost past: the bloody struggles of human history generally and of the Hidehira clan specifically. Issa's haiku, substituting poppies for Bashō's grass, could suggest (as mentioned earlier) that a peaceful era has replaced a violent one. However, more broadly, he might be suggesting that in every era, every place, gentle flowers will thrive in the wake of violence and destruction. To use the terminology of Chinese Taoism with which Issa would have been familiar, the ravages of human history caused by the active, violent, male principle of yang ultimately must give way to the patient, peaceful, female principle of yin. In the end, Issa invites us to hope, the flowers will prevail.[31]

A more comic poem, this one of uncertain composition date, reveals the same association of warrior with destructive violence. Issa warns a cuckoo not to disturb a sleeping samurai.

そっと鳴け隣は武士ぞ時鳥 (? ; *IZ* 1.347)
sotto nake tonari wa bushi zo hototogisu

> sing soft!
> a samurai lives next door
> cuckoo

Issa humorously implies that the testy samurai might unleash his wrath upon the small, warbling bird: an absurd exaggeration that satirically exposes an unsettling reality of an era in which members of the warrior class exercised un-checked authority over members of lower ranked classes. By law, a merchant or peasant who disrespected a samurai (in the samurai's opinion) could be murdered on the spot, and rumors of samurai testing new blades by decapitating random passers-by—whether true or not—gave commoners ample reason to fear and avoid these men whose social role, ironically, was to protect them. In theory, samurai followed a code of *messhi hōkō* 滅私奉公: "sacrifice of self in service to the public" (Prasol 87). In reality, they most often resorted to violent action in service of their personal sense of honor, the usual punishment for disrespect by a member of an inferior class being death by *kirisute* 切り捨て: a compound of "cut" (*kiri*) and "throw away" (*sute*; 98). Taking swift revenge for any perceived insult was not only expected but praiseworthy behavior for a samurai (Yamamoto 30; 171). Issa's comic warning to the singing cuckoo prompts a smile while calling attention to a real and frightening danger in Tokugawa Japan.

Perhaps surprisingly, in other poetic portraits Issa invites sympathy for sword-wielding samurai. In the following haiku the imbalance of power between a warrior and a bird remains, but their roles are now reversed.

> 武士や鶯に迄つかはるる (1813; *IZ* 1.133)
> *samurai ya uguisu ni made tsukawaruru*

> samurai—
> even the nightingale
> gives orders

Samurai had to bow to their superiors, following a difficult and stringent code of behavior (*bushidō* 武士道). If their rank was low, they did this for little pay. If Makoto Ueda is correct in picturing a caged bird in the scene (96), it must belong to a feudal lord, and the samurai must have been charged with the lowly chores of feeding it and cleaning its cage. On one level, Issa again is writing comedy: a poetic sketch of a powerful swordsman humbled by a tiny songbird. On a deeper level—a level that the devoted reader of Issa soon comes to expect—the haiku calls attention to the samurai's humanity. The man tending the cuckoo appears not a demonized agent of destruction but instead, like everyone else below the rank of shogun, a victim of the Tokugawa era's rigid social hierarchy. Readers may chuckle at the notion of a samurai receiving his marching orders from a bird, but, at the same time, the absurdity of the scene portrayed in the haiku exposes the oppressiveness of Japanese social structure and invites sympathy for all those trapped within it, including samurai.

Three years later, in 1816, Issa returns to this theme of a humbled samurai with another comic image charged with deeper implications.

> 武士に蝿を追する御馬哉 (1816; *IZ* 1.374)
> *samurai ni hae wo owasuru o-uma kana*
>
> the samurai is ordered
> to shoo the flies...
> Sir Horse

In translating this haiku, I have chosen to picture a single fly-shooing samurai, but Issa's language also permits readers to imagine the perhaps even funnier scene of a whole retinue of samurai lined up to service and brush the flies off "Sir Horse"; this is how French translator Jean Cholley envisions it (145). As in the previous poem, Issa satirically depicts a samurai as the servant of a privileged animal: he serves a daimyo's nightingale in the first case; he serves a daimyo's horse in the second. In other haiku, Issa shows that even the top-ranked samurai, the daimyo, can ironically become an animal's servant.

大名のなでてやりけり馬の汗 (1803; *IZ* 1.294)
daimyō no nadete yari keri uma no ase

the great lord
does the brushing . . .
horse's sweat

大将が馬をあをぐや白扇 (1823; *IZ* 1.311)
ōshō ga uma wo aogu ya shira ōgi

the general cools off
his horse . . .
white paper fan

Here the role reversal is even more extreme. Instead of a lower ranked samurai tending to the horse, the powerful figure who fans it is identified as a daimyo in the first poem and, in the second, an *ōshō* 大将, a word that in Issa's time designated a warlord or daimyo. On summer days ("sweat" and "fan" being summer season words), the lords in question kindly brush and cool their horses. The scenes repeat the image of a warrior servicing an animal, but this time the underlying message is somewhat different than in the previous examples. In those scenes, the nightingale and the horse embodied the authority of a social superior; the subservient samurai was following orders, respecting hierarchy, and, as we have seen, drawing attention to the sometimes humiliating consequences of feudal structure. In these examples, however, the daimyo in the scenes are not brushing and fanning the horses in accordance with some more highly ranked person's command. Instead, they seem to be motivated purely by their own sense of compassion for a fellow creature and friend. Perhaps not by chance, the following haiku appears immediately prior to the second example in Issa's journal, *Hachiban nikki.*

蝶の身も業の秤にかかる哉 (1817; *IZ* 1.171)
chō no mi mo gō no hakari ni kakaru kana

the butterfly too
on the scales of karma
is weighed

Issa must have been fond of this haiku, originally written in 1817, judging by the many times he recopied it in his journals, including *Hachiban nikki* in a Fifth Month entry for 1823, preceding his haiku portrait of the warlord fanning the horse. Butterflies, horses, and even generals, Issa suggests, will all be weighed on the same scales of karma: an allusion to Emma (Yama), the Judge of Hell, who gauges the karma of each new entrant to the Buddhist hell by means of scales that indicate the degree and nature of their punishments.[32] Significantly, Issa prefaces this haiku in one text with the head note, "Emma Temple," a reference to any one of several temples in Japan (including those in Kamakura and Kyoto) dedicated to hell's judge. In the haiku that follows this one in Issa's journal, the image of a general fanning his horse drives home the idea that the man in question, despite his lofty and powerful social position, is just a man and, even deeper than that, just a creature among other creatures: not their superior but a fellow traveler on the road to Buddhist enlightenment.

Issa writes several haiku that shed light on the underlying humanity of samurai, especially in connection with the beauty of the natural universe and the natural human response to it. In an autumn scene depicting a harvest moon-viewing party, a samurai sits shoulder-to-shoulder with fellow representatives of Tokugawa era society.

> 名月や出家士諸商人 (1821; *IZ* 1.459)
> *meigetsu ya shukke samurai shoakindo*
>
> harvest moon-gazing
> priests, samurai
> merchants

Representatives of three major social groups of early modern Japan unite under the moon, and although Issa leaves out the peasant class, this most populous group is also present in the scene, since the observing and, presumably, participating poet came, as we know, from a farming family. The haiku proposes a vision in which social differences are dissolved by the shimmering beauty in the sky. Japanese society is at least temporarily redefined in the haiku to express a radical equality among human beings in their ability to appreciate this universe's splendor. A year later, in 1822, Issa writes a springtime haiku that might be viewed as a companion poem of this one.

> 花の世や出家士諸商人 (1822; *IZ* 1.219)
> *hana no yo ya shukke samurai shoakindo*
>
> world of blossoms—
> priests, samurai
> merchants

In these complementary haiku samurai appear alongside and on a par with members of other social classes, reveling in the autumn moon above, the spring blossoms below.
In another haiku of that same year, Issa depicts a samurai at a flower-viewing party.

侍にてうし持たせて菊の花 (1822; *IZ* 1.562)
samurai ni chōshi motasete kiku no hana

letting the samurai
hold the sake dipper . . .
chrysanthemums

The poem alludes to an Eighth Month chrysanthemum-viewing gathering in which rice wine lubricates the festivities. Someone (the host, perhaps) has invited a samurai to hold the sake dipper and, one imagines, to fill and refill the cups of guests. Nature—more specifically, natural beauty—again serves as a kind of social leveler, dissolving human-made distinctions of status and power. Echoing the earlier example of poppies growing where warriors once walked, the "yang" violence normally associated with samurai has yielded to the gentle "yin" power of flowers.

Many contemporary literary critics and magazine editors consider haiku to be unworthy of their attention due to the mistaken assumption that the brevity of the genre precludes the serious development of poetic ideas. However, as we have seen in the present examination of Issa's samurai haiku as well as in our previous discussion of his haiku about children, farmers, and priests; one way for a master of one-breath poetry to achieve thematic depth is to attack the same matter repeatedly via a barrage of different images. Surface details may change, but the deeper semantics of these related poems resonate with and build upon one another, gradually deepening the reader's insights. The following haiku is another example of this method.

侍が傘さしかけるぼたん哉 (1818; *IZ* 1.395)
samurai ga kasa sashikakeru botan kana

> shaded by the
> samurai's umbrella . . .
> the peony

Instead of a sword the warrior in the scene wields, with a delicate sentiment of concern and protectiveness, an umbrella. Again Issa humanizes his samurai, showing that this particular one loves and cares about a flower, spontaneously exhibiting *jihi* 慈悲, compassion. Perhaps surprisingly to some readers, he has a heart. The surface details of poems may change, showing a warrior holding an umbrella over a peony in one haiku, serving sake at a chrysanthemum party in another, fanning a horse or gazing at the moon; but Issa's theme throughout these connected verses remains constant and grows forceful through repetition. Ultimately, the samurai in Issa's poetic vision is human; he is us.

In one haiku Issa dramatically portrays even one of the highest ranked samurai, a daimyo, appreciating nature.

> 大名を馬からおろす桜哉 (1824; *IZ* 1.234)
> *daimyō wo uma kara orosu sakura kana*
>
> the war lord
> forced off his horse . . .
> cherry blossoms

The poem is prefaced with a place name, "Ueno." In addition to being a famous locale for viewing cherry blossoms, Ueno is a site where the first Tokugawa shogun, Ieyasu, is enshrined (in addition to his more elaborate shrine at Nikko). As Japanese critic Maruyama Kazuhiko points out, in Issa's day, out of respect for the first shogun's shrine, a "Dismount Your Horse" placard was posted at the foot of Ueno Hill (344). Perhaps then, Maruyama suggests, the daimyo in the scene is simply obeying this sign, dismounting before continuing up the hill on his blossom-viewing excursion.

Whether or not the daimyo has indeed seen such a sign, the poem presents a surprising reversal of expectations. The lord of the province enacts a gesture of humility before "mere" blossoms. The great American Japanologist, Harold Gould Henderson, also weighs in on this particular poem in *An Introduction to Haiku*. Henderson feels that the haiku might allude to the protocol of the period, which required commoners to grovel by the roadside whenever a daimyo passed (128). Here, the blossoms surprisingly represent a higher authority to which even a daimyo must bow. In this remarkable haiku Issa not only repeats the motif of a man of war appreciating nature's delicate beauty; he slyly suggests that this beauty, owned by no one and existing beyond the system of the human social ranking, outranks a daimyo.

In the next poems, two more role-reversal haiku about daimyo, nature again appears as a superior power. However, in these scenes it isn't nature's beauty at play but rather its ability to inflict hardship.

> づぶ濡れの大名を見る炬燵哉 (1820; *IZ* 1.703)
> *zubunure no daimyō wo miru kotatsu kana*

> watching a war lord
> drenched . . .
> my cozy brazier

> 大名を眺ながらに炬燵哉 (1823; *IZ* 1.703)
> *daimyō wo nagame nagara ni kotatsu kana*

> eyeing the war lord
> from my toasty warm
> brazier

A cold winter rain bears down mercilessly on the military leader, who has certainly, similarly, borne down oppressively upon the people beneath him, especially the impoverished, over-taxed peasants of the land. However, here again nature rules, and the daimyo must bow to its relentless, icy authority. As an added twist to these mischievously iconoclastic poems, the poor poet—literally a nobody according to the official classes recognized in Tokugawa Japan—seems far better off than the mighty lord. While the latter travels under the winter rain, the poet observes the gray, miserable scene from the cozy warmth of his *kotatsu* 炬燵: a brazier with quilts covering and pleasantly heating his feet and legs. Issa's point could be that nature has the power to rearrange human assignments of prestige. In this moment at least, the happy poet, Shinano Province's Chief Beggar, appears more privileged than the great lord of Shinano—thanks to the downpour.

In a final example of a haiku about a samurai, Issa strikes an exceedingly tender note.

> おく霜のたしに捨たる髻哉 (1816; *IZ* 1.651)
> *oku shimo no tashi ni sutetaru tabusa kana*
>
> adding to the frost
> the samurai's discarded
> topknot

The poem, written in Twelfth Month, has this brief prose preface in *Shichiban nikki*: "White hair falls twice" (*IZ* 3.463). An elderly samurai parts with his topknot, the visible sign of his social status, on a cold winter morning. Issa's prescript might be unnecessary for most readers, but by including it he clearly doesn't want anyone to miss the fact that two white things have fallen to the ground on this frigid morning: a samurai's severed topknot and the frost. The scene recalls a long tradition in Japanese literature of a character dramatically cutting off his or her hair to represent an abrupt and total break with the past. In Tokugawa society the topknot symbolized a samurai's role: to cut it off thus signaled an irrevocable decision to abandon that role and to adopt another: to become a Buddhist monk, for example, or perhaps to work in the fields as a peasant. In Issa's time it was not uncommon for samurai to trade their higher status for the lower one of farmers because this meant, especially in hard times, at least the prospect of eating.

By emphasizing the whiteness of the hair Issa conjures an image of an old man who, for whatever reason, will or can no longer fulfill the duties and enjoy the privileges of his station. With its imagery of coldness, winter, whiteness (the death color in East Asian traditions), and severed hair (hair being a symbol of life and vigor); the haiku calls attention to the aging process and hints at what will follow. Nearing the end of his life, the samurai abandons his social role to reveal a naked truth that remains: he is just a human being looking forward now to a winter that metaphorically signifies his death. The reader is free to imagine the possible circumstances that might have led this man to end his samurai existence. If he is becoming a priest, the scene conveys a message of leaving one's social usefulness behind to strive for detachment and spiritual enlightenment. If he is becoming a peasant, the scene suggests that hunger and deprivation have precipitated a desperate redefining of his social role. If he has absolutely no future plans or prospects—if the reader chooses to imagine that the old samurai has simply grown too old to fulfill his duties in an era without social security or pensions, the scene is especially sad. However one decides to imagine it, Issa brilliantly evokes with just a few words and simple images the vulnerable, mortal man beneath the armor.[33]

Though some of his haiku portraits critique the dangerousness of samurai, Issa more typically presents a deeper perception of these men.[34] He shows them bowing to animals. He shows them mingling with other social classes to view and appreciate the autumn moon and spring's blossoms. He shows high-ranked daimyo humbling themselves to horses and cherry blossoms, and drenched by the superior power of a cold winter rain. And he shows them ultimately facing the same realities of aging and death that all creatures must face. Being human, Issa suggests, is noticeable in moments when class differences dissolve, when social role is severed like a samurai's topknot, and when people open their hearts and minds to a universe of nature and fellow creatures with an attitude of acceptance and appreciation. Where fearsome warriors once trod, Issa promises, poppies will grow.

Chapter 5. ARTISANS AND MERCHANTS

In Japan's early modern period—the so-called Tokugawa or Edo era of 1603-1868—the old feudal power relations among social classes shifted dramatically due to the rise of a vigorous, urban-based capitalism that included sophisticated financial and marketing systems. Many merchants became rich; many samurai became poor. Nevertheless, merchants continued to occupy the lowest position in the shogunate's official four-class hierarchy of samurai, farmer, artisan, and merchant—based on a Neo-Confucian value system that viewed them "as producing nothing yet making a profit off the labor of others" (Deal 112). Ieyasu Tokugawa, the first shogun, declared that any inferior person who disrespects a superior can be treated "like a merchant," suggesting the disdain with which samurai viewed this class of people (Prasol 98). Residing mostly in towns and cities, merchants and artisans were referred to collectively as "townspeople" (*chōnin* 町人) by the samurai (Deal 114): social inferiors who, ironically, often were richer than their samurai overlords. The growing power of money in Japan's urban centers did not go unnoticed by Issa, who in an interesting haiku of 1824 draws an improbable equal sign between the nation and the accumulation of interest.

日の本や金も子をうむ御代の春 (1824; *IZ* 1.27)
hi no moto ya kane mo ko wo umu miyo no haru

Land of the Rising Sun!
money makes money . . .
the emperor's spring

The seasonal reference, "emperor's spring" (*miyo no haru* 御代の春), refers to New Year's Day, the start of a new year of the emperor's reign. In Japan, the "Land of the Rising Sun (*hi no moto* 日の本), Issa notes, "money makes money." More literally, he claims that "money, too, gives birth to children." The "too" (*mo*) is significant, though I purposefully have left it out of my translation in an attempt at creating a stronger haiku in English. Money has babies *too*, Issa writes, just like people—thus oddly anthropomorphizing capital. A new calendar year, he notes, signals a bit more interest due to lenders, a bit more burden of debt for borrowers. Money, invisibly, has reproduced itself. New Year's day in Issa's time occurred around mid-February of the modern calendar, so New Year's Day also was the start of spring—buds in the trees promising new life about to burst into bloom. Ironically, the first blooming of spring in *this* poem is the birth of more money in the Land of the Rising Sun.

Is Issa being satirical and therefore critical of the new direction that Japan is taking, a direction that later will lead to gleaming, earthquake-proof skyscrapers housing financial institutions towering above Tokyo and Osaka? The reader is free to answer this question for him or herself, but I choose to read satire and dark criticism in this New Year's poem for two reasons. The first has to do with the placement of the haiku in Issa's journal, *Bunsei kuchō* ("Bunsei Era Haiku Collection"). Issa composed it in Twelfth Month of 1824, but decided to recopy it as the second haiku of First Month, 1825 (*IZ* 4.519; 4.525). The preceding poem of that year offers a revealing contrast.

神国や草も元日きつと咲 (1825; *IZ* 1.53)
kamiguni ya kusa mo ganjitsu kitto saku

country of gods!
on New Year's Day grasses
suddenly bloom

The "country of gods" is Japan, homeland of the Shinto deities (*kami* 神). This nation, Issa suggests, is so devout that even its grasses are blooming with wildflowers in honor of the gods on spring's first day. Immediately after this poem, Issa repeats the haiku written a month earlier: "Land of the Rising Sun!/ money makes money . . ./ the emperor's spring." This artificial spring "blooming" with profit contrasts significantly with the natural blooming of the divinely blessed grasses. Although Lewis Mackenzie believed that Issa may have been referring to "some cherished pot-plant" (45), the grass in the poem is more likely *fukuju kusa* 福寿草: "prosperity grass" or "longevity grass," a New Year's season word.[35] By consciously recopying his poem about blooming profit in the New Year's 1825 section of his journal, immediately following and pointedly contrasting with his opening poem about blooming grasses, Issa invites the reader to contemplate an important difference. Both haiku are sweeping statements about Japan—a "country of gods" in the first and "Land of the Rising Sun" in the second—but their images directly clash. In the first, grasses bloom freely, and their blooming is presented as a sacred thing. In the second, money gives birth to money—a shift from the natural world to human society, from a blessing for all to a blessing for only the fortunate and a curse for those who owe money to the fortunate. Nature is pure and, in Shinto understanding, divine; the human world, in contrast, is materialistic and governed by egoistical (hence, un-Buddhist) self-interest. The "money makes money" haiku's placement in Issa's journal could therefore suggest both irony and social criticism.

A second reason for reading social critique in this poem is that Issa developed and projected in his work the self-persona of an impoverished "Chief Beggar of Shinano Province."

<blockquote>
三寸の胸ですむ也店おろし (1823; *IZ* 1.35)
san-zun no mune de sumu nari tana oroshi

there's so little
I do it in my head . . .
New Year's inventory
</blockquote>

The *tana oroshi* 店おろし is a New Year's inventory during which merchants examine their stock and enter its value into account books (*Kogo daijiten* 1,013). Issa's assets are so few, he humorously reports in this haiku, he can do his entire inventory in his head.[36] The poem asserts the poet's poverty and lack of assets. A reader who keeps this and similar haiku in mind while reflecting on Issa's "money makes money" poem might conclude that all of this nation-wide money-making doesn't help the poor of the land, including the beggarly poet. In fact, as owners of more debt than capital, Issa and the poor find themselves poorer on the year's first day, not richer.

Merchants, it bears repeating, are among the happy viewers of spring blossoms and autumn moon in two previously cited haiku.

<blockquote>
花の世や出家士諸商人 (1822; *IZ* 1.219)
hana no yo ya shukke samurai shoakindo

world of blossoms—
priests, samurai
merchants

名月や出家士諸商人 (1821; IZ 1.459)
meigetsu ya shukke samurai shoakindo
</blockquote>

harvest moon-gazing
priests, samurai
merchants

In these poems Issa implies that members of various social classes, including the money-making class, bow in unison to the higher, more sublime power of nature and natural beauty—freely available to all and, as his haiku about the "country of gods" reminds us, divinely infused.

In addition to the merchants who were amassing fortunes in early modern Japan, a wide variety of artisans and small-time vendors appear in Issa's poetic portraits, including sellers of umbrella-hats, bamboo blinds, sugar, flowers, vegetables, winnows, cotton, tea-cakes, pickles, tofu, sandals, rice cakes, sake, sardines, dumplings, katydids, and toy flutes. In all of these haiku, the act of selling is closely and significantly tied to nature and to season. In some, the natural context seems harsh and forbidding.

朝寒し寒しと菜うり箕うり哉 (1805; *IZ* 1.433)
asa samushi samushi to nauri miuri kana

so cold in morning's cold—
vegetable vendor
winnow vendor

はつ霜や並ぶ花売鉦たたき (1815; *IZ* 1.650)
hatsu shimo ya narabu hanauri kane tataki

first frost—
flower sellers in a row
hitting their bells

The vendors in these examples occupy a low rung on the ladder of capitalism, and Issa's sympathy for them is palpable. In the first poem he repeats the word "cold" (*samushi* 寒し), thereby emphasizing the bitter, low temperature that the sellers of vegetables and winnows must endure. The second haiku, set on winter's first frosty morning, is poignant. The flower vendors bang their bells with greater urgency, given the onset of wintry weather, desperate to sell their stock before it freezes. The beginning of winter has arrived: a period of physical danger for all who have not provided for themselves. Each clang of their bells is a plaintive appeal for their very survival.

Other haiku about selling goods in bitter-cold weather also suggest, without outright stating, a feeling of commiseration.

> わらじ売窓に朝寒始りぬ (1816; *IZ* 1.433)
> *waraji uru mado ni asa-zamu hajimarinu*
>
> a sandal vendor
> at the window, morning's
> cold beginning
>
> 猫の穴から物をかふ寒さ哉 (1822; *IZ* 1.609)
> *neko no ana kara mono wo kau samusa kana*
>
> buying from the vendor
> through the cat's door . . .
> it's cold!

On a winter morning the door-to-door sandal artisan-vendor arrives at a window (presumably Issa's), showing his wares. Once again the coldness of the natural setting symbolically suggests the coldness of a social system in which one's survival depends on finding buyers for one's goods. The second haiku, more comic in tone, again describes an encounter between a potential customer (probably Issa) and a traveling vendor. It's so cold outside, the customer refuses to open the door but instead crouches low to complete the transaction through the cat's door. The scene is funny but might also lead the reader to reflect on the vendor's hard way of life: the necessity of plying his trade on a day too cold for his fellow citizens to venture outside, or even to open their doors.

In other haiku Issa links the activity of merchants to happier, more optimistic natural and seasonal events, such as the springtime blooming of flowers.

素湯売りも久しくなるや花の山 (1805; *IZ* 1.209)
sayu uri mo hisashiku naru ya hana no yama

even the hot water vendor
lingers . . .
blossoming mountain

とうふ屋が来る昼顔が咲にけり (1810; *IZ* 1.390)
tōfu ya ga kuru hirugao ga saki ni keri

the tofu vendor comes—
the day flower
blooms

The vendor in the first example has hot water to sell, but the spring blossoms covering a mountain (or mountains) cause him to neglect his work for a while. He "too" (*mo*)—like other people in the scene—lingers to soak up nature's splendor. In the second example, Issa comically suggests that the tofu vendor comes around so regularly, like clockwork, he in fact functions as a clock. The *hirugao* (literally, "noon faces") are delicate pink and white blooms of bindweed that open in the day and close at dusk. Literally, Issa asserts that "the day flowers of the vendor's coming have bloomed." The vendor's rounds are thus perceived to align with nature's cycles, suggesting that the door-to-door selling of tofu is part of nature too—not a separate, alien or alienating activity.

The merchant arriving and the flower opening form part of a greater harmony.

In this next haiku about a vendor among spring blossoms, Issa plays skillfully with sound.

> がらがらやぴいぴいうりや梅の花 (1817; *IZ* 1.200)
> *gara-gara ya pii-pii uri ya ume no hana*
>
> the toy flute seller
> clatters along . . .
> plum blossoms

The vendor sells *pii-pii* ぴいぴい, an onomatopoetic word for children's toy flutes. He enters the scene with a clatter (perhaps of his wares?) described with another Japanese onomatopoetic term, *gara-gara*. The combination of *gara-gara* and *pii-pii* establishes a happy mood that perfectly accords with the capping image of blooming plum. Again, the human activity of selling appears as an essential part of a springtime day in Japan, on planet Earth, in a universe that creates and sustains it all, including blooming plum trees and toy flute sellers.

In the following haiku, cherry blossoms provide a welcome distraction from commerce.

> 団子など商ひながら花見哉 (1821; *IZ* 1.217)
> *dango nado akinai nagara hanami kana*
>
> while selling his dumplings
> and such . . .
> blossom viewing

> 畠縁りに酒を売也花盛 (1818; *IZ* 1.215)
> *hata-beri ni sake wo uru nari hana-zakari*

>   at the field's edge
>   a sake vendor . . .
>   glorious blossoms

A man sells dumplings "and such" (*nado* など) but does not devote his full attention to this gainful activity. Even while he works, he looks up to gaze at blossoms, presumably cherry blossoms. In the other thematically similar poem, a vendor has set up at the edge of a field to sell sake to farmers during their work breaks. Once again, we might imagine that the man's mind is not exclusively devoted to his selling, since the nearby cherry blossoms have reached their absolute "peak" (*sakari* 盛) of glory. In all the above examples, Issa presents vendors immersed in, and appreciating, the beauty of this world's flowers and blossoms.

In a poem about a pickle vendor, the seasonal context is a spring downpour.

> 春雨や千代の古道菜漬売 (1806; *IZ* 1.68)
> *harusame ya chiyo no furu michi nazuke uri*
>
> spring rain
> on an ancient road . . .
> the pickle vendor

Issa again presents the itinerant vendor as an integral part of a greater harmony consisting, in this case, of nature—as embodied in the pouring-down spring rain—and of human history—represented by the "ancient road" or "old road" (*furu michi* 古道) on which he travels. This seller of *nazuke*, pickled vegetables, appears as the centerpiece of a complex poetic image that evokes ideas of newness (spring rain) alongside oldness (the road). The soaked vendor thus can be thought to exist both now and forever: as a unique individual in this particular moment of time and as an archetype for all time. The reader might sympathize somewhat with his need to travel, hence work, in the rain, but the image isn't tragic or pitiful. The pickle vendor is simply part of the picture, part of spring and part of the ongoing human story from ancient times to the present.

Two haiku about sandal vendors are also quite complex and evocative in their imagery.

> 作りながらわらぢ売なり木下闇 (1821; *IZ* 1.421)
> *tsukuri nagara waraji uru nari ko shita yami*
>
> making straw sandals
> while selling them . . .
> deep tree shade
>
> わらぢ売る木陰の爺が清水哉 (? ; *IZ* 1.277)
> *waraji uru kokage no jiji ga shimizu kana*
>
> selling straw sandals
> in the shade, an old man . . .
> pure water

Both poems are set in summer. In the first, a vendor escapes the heat of the day in cool tree shade while accomplishing, simultaneously, both the manufacturing and selling of his product. Issa presents the industrious artisan as part of the natural scene rather than as an intruder in it. The relative darkness under the trees, however, invites readers to imagine a subdued mood and to wonder if Issa might perhaps be suggesting a sense of sadness in this image of hard-working, never-resting artisan-vendor. The second poem also has summer shade as its season word or *kigo*. This time, the sandal vendor is old, but contrasting to his age is the image of pure, gushing spring water, evoking for readers a green mountain setting. Nature is vast, ancient, and eternally renewing itself (or, in Western mythology, *her*self). Human beings live, labor, and die quickly in comparison with the great whole. Issa's haiku portrait of an old artisan selling footwear that he has presumably woven himself, after a lifetime of doing this same work day in and day out, invites the reader to wonder and to contemplate. Is the scene happy or sad? Have all those busy years of labor been worth it in the grand scheme of things? This masterful haiku, through its strategically constructed and evocatively interesting images—deep shade, pure water, sandal-selling old man—opens a world of questions. However one chooses ultimately to answer them, Issa clearly honors the old vendor by considering his situation intently and by sharing that consideration with readers, inviting them to reflect deeply on what his life might mean and might have meant.

In another haiku about vendors selling their wares under summer trees, Issa strikes a more comic tone.

屁のやうな茶もうれる也夏木立 (1816; *IZ* 1.419)
he no yōna cha mo ureru nari natsu kodachi

they even sell tea
not worth a fart!
summer trees

The Japanese expression, *he no yōna* 屁のやうな—literally, "fart-like"—metaphorically signifies "worthless," though Issa might be humorously suggesting that the tea *literally* smells like flatulence. In either case, the tea has been decidedly a bad purchase, and Issa's haiku reads like a consumer's complaint. In this atypical poem, his attitude toward the vendor is not one of understanding or compassion but of indignation at being cheated.

In two haiku Issa writes about mechanical vendors: the Edo-period forerunners of twenty first-century robot workers.

人形に餅を売らせて夕涼 (1818; *IZ* 1.323)
ningyō ni mochi wo urasete yūsuzumi

making the doll
sell rice cakes . . .
evening cool

人形に茶をはこばせて門涼み (1819; *IZ* 1.324)
ningyō ni cha wo hakobasete kado suzumi

a doll is made
to bring my tea . . .
cool air at the gate

The second poem has the headnote, "Doll Street" 人形町, referring to an area of Edo where mechanical dolls were featured (Kobayashi Issa, *The Year of My Life* 55). In these verses Issa playfully showcases an aspect of marketing that perhaps has always been part of capitalism: the attraction of customers by means of a gimmick. In these pleasant scenes of cool summer evenings the merchants behind the machines stay hidden, but we can imagine that the novelty of their mechanical doll-waitresses has substantially increased the day's profit.

Earlier we examined a haiku that depicts a sake vendor serving farmers in their fields in springtime. Issa also has poems about such vendors working during summer's barley harvest.

麦秋や子を負ながらいはし売 (1819; *IZ* 1.407)
mugi aki ya ko wo oi nagara iwashiuri

ripened barley—
with a child on her back
the sardine vendor

麦秋や畠を歩く小酒うり (1824; *IZ* 1.407)
mugi aki ya hatake wo aruku ko sake uri

ripened barley—
walking through the field
a little sake vendor

Mugi 麦 is a generic term that refers to several grains: wheat, barley, oats, and rye. The seasonal expression with which Issa begins these two haiku, *mugi aki* 麦秋 ("barley's autumn"), is so called because summer's harvest of *mugi* visually resembles the rice harvest of autumn. In the first poem the grain is mature and ready for harvest, a death image, while the baby bundled on his or her mother's or older sister's back can symbolically suggest the beginning of life. Not mentioned in the haiku, but implied, are the field workers to whom the mother or sister sells her sardines. If imagined assiduously, the haiku presents a scene teeming with life: a field of golden grain, hungry harvesters, a mother or older sister, a child. The act of selling, as so often is the case in Issa's poetry, appears as an integral and harmonious part of a natural setting. The second haiku shows a child vendor in the same setting, walking through a field selling drinks of sake to the farmers. There is no hint of disapproval at the adult exploitation of child labor in the scene.[57] The little merchant, though young, appears in the poem as simply an active participant in a busy, happy, agrarian scene.

A haiku about the selling of a living thing is less happy.

きりぎりす身を売れても鳴にけり (1820; *IZ* 1.549)
kirigirisu mi wo urarete mo naki ni keri

the katydid—
even while they sell him
singing

A cousin of crickets and grasshoppers, the male *kirigirisu* or katydid produces shrill mating calls with special organs on his wings. Issa's image of a caged katydid continuing to sing despite the hopelessness of his situation evokes sympathy, especially when one takes into account the poet's lifelong concern for, and ability to imagine the experiential point of view of, animals. Because the reader is invited to feel sorry for the insect, he or she might at the same time feel anger toward the human beings who have made him into a commodity: mere merchandise that provides amusement for buyers, profit for sellers, but torment (along with the almost certain probability of dying alone and mate-less) for the katydid. The poem might therefore be read as an indictment of a human society that values private profit over the welfare of fellow creatures.

A haiku written that same year four months later (Eighth Month), also has satirical bite.

銭箱の穴より出たりきりぎりす (1820; *IZ* 1.549)
zeni-bako no ana yori detari kirigirisu

from the hole
in the money box . . .
a katydid

In this example of bait-and-switch humor, which we have noted was a favorite rhetorical pattern for Issa, the reader's expectation is confounded at the end of the poem when a katydid rather than coins comes out of the box. The insect literally has replaced money, prompting a sympathetic groan or chuckle at someone's (probably Issa's) poverty. On a deeper level, the haiku calls into question the true value of life, however small. Is the singing autumn insect perhaps, in a real sense, more precious than coins? In other haiku Issa spoofs the human habit of placing price tags on living things, including grass, blossoms, and water that should be free for all to enjoy. Since he often situates these poems in Edo and Kyoto, they particularly serve to satirize the money-grubbing ways of large cities.

> 青草も銭だけそよぐ門涼 (1819; *IZ* 1.323)
> *ao-gusa mo zeni dake soyogu kado suzumi*
>
> even green grass
> rustles only for money...
> cool air at the gate
>
> 江戸桜花も銭だけ光る哉 (1820; *IZ* 1.232)
> *edo sakura hana mo zeni dake hikaru kana*
>
> Edo's cherry blossoms, too
> shine only
> for money
>
> 月かげや夜も水売る日本橋 (1822; *IZ* 1.330)
> *tsukikage ya yoru mo mizu uru nihombashi*
>
> moonlight—
> even at night they sell water
> on Nihon Bridge
>
> 花見るも銭をとらるる都哉 (1824; *IZ* 1.220)
> *hana miru mo zeni wo toraruru miyako kana*
>
> even viewing the cherry blossoms
> costs money...
> Kyoto

Issa prefaces the first example with the headnote, "Living in Edo." Everything is for sale, it seems, in the shogun's city, even rustling grasses—suggesting that the scene might be unfolding in a private garden. The second example, in which

Edo's blossoms "too" (*mo*) "shine only for money," also seems set in a private garden that blossom-gazers can enter and enjoy only after paying an entrance fee. In the third example, set on Nihon Bridge in the heart of old Edo, even a simple drink of water has a price. Finally, the fourth example notes that the emperor's city of Kyoto also requires tourists to pay to view its blossoms. In all of these haiku (and many more that could be cited), the word "even" or "too" (*mo*) suggests a lament: the normally, ideally free gifts of nature such as grass, water, and blossoms *also* carry price tags in Japan's great commercial centers—and, it deserves mentioning, in certain tourist-trap villages as well:

一里の身すぎの桜咲にけり (1805; *IZ* 1.224)
hito sato no misugi no sakura saki ni keri

it's how the village
makes a living . . .
cherry trees in bloom

In some poems Issa links the selling of nature's bounty to the current age of corruption as defined by Pure Land Buddhism.

今の世や蛇の衣も銭になる (1825; *IZ* 1.354)
ima no yo ya hebi no koromo mo zeni ni naru

the world today!
even a snake's skin
for sale

一本は桜もちけり娑婆の役 (1809; *IZ* 1.226)
ippon wa sakura mochi keri shaba no yaku

> one cherry tree
> has kept blooming . . .
> the corrupt world

According to Shinran and other Pure Land patriarchs, the present age of *mappō* 末法 is one of deeply rooted, ego-fueled corruption, so much so that people are incapable of achieving Buddhist awakening by their own self-powered efforts and thus require the Other Power of Amida Buddha. Issa interestingly connects the selling of snakeskins to "the world today" (*ima no yo* 今の世), a phrase that specifically refers to the lamentable current age in a Pure Land Buddhist understanding. The image is especially effective because a snake's skin-shedding can be viewed as a Buddhist symbol for discarding worldly corruption and moving toward awakening. Ironically, this symbol of Buddhist progression becomes here an object used in Buddhist retrogression, as a vendor has decided to sell it for his own private, ego-serving profit; literally, the snake's skin "turns into money." The second example, written fourteen years earlier (1809), pointedly relates the "corrupt world" to a particular blooming cherry tree. Though less explicit than the image of a snake's skin becoming money, the linking of a cherry tree to the current age of depravity can be interpreted as yet another jab at Tokugawa period capitalism. The person (or persons) who own the tree in question is profiting from it—perhaps charging admission to a garden or perhaps selling local goods to swarms of blossom tourists. Cherry blossoms, like a snake's shed skin, also convey traditionally symbolic meaning in a Buddhist context, for they suggest the Buddha's tenet that everything in this world is transitory. The beauty of blossoms, for so short a spell, reminds one that all life, all things, are temporary—a necessary insight on the road to the end of suffering and spiritual awakening. Once again, corrupt, acquisitive humans ironically squeeze ego-pleasing profit from a natural phenomenon that ideally should lead them away from worldliness, if only perceived correctly.

In similar fashion, several of Issa's haiku portraits show Buddhist temples, spiritual institutions meant to lead the faithful away from mundane attachments, engaged in worldly profit-seeking. Examples of this abound; the following are typical.

十月やほのぼのかすむ御綿売 (1810; *IZ* 1.605)
jūgatsu ya honobono kasumu o-wata uri

first winter month—
dimly in the mist
selling temple cotton

堂守りが茶菓子売る也夏木立 (1815; *IZ* 1.419)
dōmori ga chagashi uru nari natsu kodachi

the temple guard
sells tea cakes . . .
grove of summer trees

花ちるや一開帳の集め銭 (1815; *IZ* 1.214)
hana chiru ya hito kaichō no atsume zeni

scattering blossoms—
money is collected
Buddha on display

金まうけ上手な寺のぼたん哉 (1825; *IZ* 1.396)
kane mōke jōzuna tera no botan kana

a money-making
temple . . .
the peonies in bloom

Since Tenth Month was the first month of winter in the old Japanese calendar, "first winter month" is a translation that captures this important fact that would have been obvious to Issa's original readers of the first haiku. This beginning-of-winter poem has a prescript, "Eighth Day, at Suidochō"—a Buddhist temple where, instead of delivering guidance away from worldly concerns, the priests are selling cotton and/or cotton items. In the second example a temple guard (*dōmori* 堂守り) sells teacakes (*chagashi* 茶菓子), suggesting that the instant that a pilgrim sets foot in the temple's precincts the frenzy of selling snacks and merchandise has (sadly) begun. The third example is perhaps the most depressing and damning: the Buddha statue of a particular temple is put on display specifically, Issa claims, to garner coins from the faithful. In the fourth example, involving a temple that evidently has a flower garden, he calls it, with biting sarcasm, "a money-making temple." It is easy to imagine Priest Issa's tone of profound disappointment.

In Issa's poetic vision, the spread of money's power throughout the Japanese archipelago meant, in Buddhist terms, an increase of ego-centered and ego-serving corruption. In one tragicomic haiku, he hints that the meticulous recording of gain and loss in account ledgers takes place even in the gloomy pits of hell.

梅折やえんまの帳につく合点 (1817; *IZ* 1.200)
ume oru ya emma no chō ni tsuku gaten

plum blossom thievery—
added to the account book
of hell's judge Emma

Emma (Yama) records the theft of plum blossoms in his infernal account book, assuring that the thief (most likely Issa) will one day be duly punished. The haiku has a light and joking tone, similar to that of an earlier poem of 1812 in which the sin of plum blossom thievery appeared in "hell's mirror."[38] By shifting Emma's recording device for sin from a magic mirror to an account book, Issa might be suggesting, beneath his poem's humor, the tragically diabolical nature of moneymaking in a Buddhist understanding. In many haiku, as we have seen, selling appears as a necessary survival tactic for poor, hard-working, long-suffering vendors. However, in fewer but significant poems such as this one, selling appears as an act of self-gratification that both reflects and adds to the corruption of the depraved Latter Days of Dharma. The judge of hell thus, quite naturally, keeps an account ledger of his own.

Issa's answer to the spiritually debilitating influence of money and profit-seeking is perhaps best viewed in the following haiku in which an account book functions not as a financial record keeper but as a physical pillow.

長き日や大福帳をかり枕 (1818; *IZ* 1.61)
nagaki hi ya daifukuchō wo kari makura

a long day—
his account book serves
as a pillow

大帳を枕としたる暑かな (1819; *IZ* 1.251)
daichō wo makura to shitaru atsusa kana

account book
for a pillow . . .
the summer heat

涼しさに大福帳を枕かな (1819; *IZ* 1.256)
suzushisa ni daifukuchō wo makura kana

in summer cool
the account book
for a pillow

Issa liked this image of account book/pillow well enough to produce three versions of it: the first set in the seasonal context of a long spring day, the second set on a hot summer day, and the third, amid cool summer breezes—most likely, evening breezes. One can picture in these poems a merchant, a merchant's apprentice, or any other participant in the rampant buying, selling, and recordkeeping of Tokugawa Japan. In these pleasant natural scenes, gain and loss are utterly forgotten while the person lies down for a rest or a nap, enjoying a long, lazy day basking in the warm sun or reveling in cool air. Nature trumps capitalism in these poems; in fact, nature places capitalism in proper perspective as merely a closed book of symbols, absolutely unimportant in comparison to the natural universe of grassy hills, fragrant pines, sparkling lakes, and vast blue heavens dotted with clouds. In fact, the only purpose of money-making and recordkeeping in such scenes is to provide a convenient head rest for a person drifting to sleep in the great outdoors. Issa's haiku about individual vendors and especially artisan-vendors are often filled with tender compassion. However, verses in which he takes aim at the overall system of early modern capitalism are savagely ironic and, in their implications, condemning. There are some things in life, Issa suggests, that money cannot, should not, buy.

Chapter 6. ENTERTAINERS

As one might expect, given the rigidly stratified social order of early modern Japan, performing artists of various types constituted a well-defined hierarchy, from street singers just a notch above ordinary beggars, all the way up to the highly accomplished and widely admired geisha musicians of the Yoshiwara and other licensed pleasure districts. The period also saw the transformation of the medieval ritual of sumo wrestling into a crowd-pleasing professional sport, top wrestlers becoming as famous and as adored by local fans for their skill as were the top-ranked geisha. Although singers, dancers, musicians, kabuki actors, Noh actors, *bunraku* puppeteers, and wrestlers didn't occupy officially recognized positions in the four-class social structure sanctioned by the shogun, they nevertheless managed to survive—and some of them, to thrive—in the culturally vibrant Edo period, using their talents to quench the public's ever-growing thirst for entertainment, thus earning their share of the wealth of the expanding Japanese economy.

Issa's haiku about contemporary entertainers include portraits of solitary "crossroad singers" (*tsuji-utai* 辻うたひ) and of pairs of "begging actors" (*manzai* 万歳) who went from town to town during the New Year's season, blessing homes by performing incantatory songs mingled with stand-up comedy. He also wrote a good number of poems about Twelfth Month singers (*sekizoro* せき候), who similarly traveled across the Japanese archipelago, performing festive celebration songs. Other performers described in Issa's notebooks include the more prestigious geisha samisen players and sumo athletes, novices and champions. Issa's haiku about performing artists show empathy for their sorrows, joys, and physical challenges, along with his enthusiastic appreciation of their talent, their dedication, and their faithful preservation of time-honored Japanese traditions.

A poem about a crossroads singer has a prose introduction, "Living in the world is made hard by mountains and rivers."

木がらしや地びたに暮るる辻うたひ (1804; *IZ* 1.631)
kogarashi ya jibita ni kururu tsuji-utai

winter wind—
a street singer at dusk
hunkers to the ground

According to the editors of Issa's collected works, the crossroads singer is a type of beggar who sings little songs by the wayside (*IZ* 2.248); Makoto Ueda adds that such singers perform "passages from famous Noh plays" (54). French translator Jean Cholley visualizes several singers in the scene (59), but I choose to present just one in my English translation because, in my opinion, a solitary person hunkering outdoors after sunset with no protection from a bitter-cold wind is a sufficiently evocative image.[39] Without stating it outright, the haiku's prescript suggests Issa's compassion for the street singer who, like common beggars, must endure the elements while crossing this world's "mountains and rivers." His life, plainly, is a hard one, yet he keeps on singing.

In a later haiku about a street singer, Issa captures a lighter moment.

辻うたひ凧も上つていたりけり (1811; *IZ* 1.45)
tsujiutai tako mo nobotte itari keri

> the street singer's
> kite also . . .
> rising and rising

Since kite-flying is a New Year's activity reserved for male children, the singer is most likely a boy, but he could be an adult behaving in a childlike manner in the moment, playfully flying a kite that rises higher and higher to the heavens. The fact that the street singer's kite rises "also" (*mo*) indicates that his is but one of a sky-full of brightly colored toys. Despite his poverty and low social status, he nevertheless takes part in the communal celebration, his kite soaring alongside those of other, richer flyers. Contemplating this happy haiku, one can imagine the poor street singer's heart—and Issa's heart—rising and rising with the kites.

Like the street singers of early modern Japan, "begging actors" (*manzai*) were itinerant entertainers, crisscrossing the nation to bring their art to small audiences, for small tips. Literally, *manzai* signifies "ten thousand years." Performing music mixed with comedy at doorways during the New Year's season, *manzai* promised ten thousand years' worth of blessings for the inhabitants of each home that they visited (Groemer 347). *Manzai* performers traveled in pairs consisting of a "master" (*tayū* 大夫) and a "wit" (*saizō* 才蔵). The master wore a courtier's hat (*ebōshi* 烏帽子) and an elaborately patterned robe to match his refined, polished, and erudite poetic style. His songs, often accompanied by strumming on his samisen while his partner the wit pounded a small drum, constituted incantations to bless the home and the people residing therein, assuring everyone's health and prosperity (364). The wit, in contrast, played the role of a joking, foul-mouthed commoner, providing a comic counterpoint to the master's serious chant. The wit's bawdy and largely improvised banter dealt with age-old stereotypes of world comedy, including foolish old men bedding young women and clueless parents who are unaware of the *real* reason that their teenage daughter's belly has been swelling lately (374).

In his haiku portraits of such performers, Issa's admiration and appreciation are evident—not surprisingly, perhaps, in light of his love for comic incongruity in his own art.

> 万歳よも一ツはやせ春の雪 (1803; *IZ* 1.47)
> *manzai yo mo hitotsu hayase haru no yuki*
>
> begging actors
> play one more song!
> spring snow
>
> 万歳のけふも昔に成りにけり (1808; *IZ* 1.47)
> *manzai no kyō mo mukashi ni nari ni keri*
>
> begging actors—
> the olden times return
> today

In the first example, Issa evokes the enthusiasm of an audience for these talented bringers of blessings. The New Year's season, consisting of New Year's Day and the following weeks, comprised the official beginning of spring. However, snow falls in the scene nonetheless, suggesting the hardiness of the traveling pair. The people of the home beg them for an encore: to endure the cold for a bit longer to perform another song. The second example constitutes a glowing compliment for the *manzai*, as Issa claims that their performance has literally turned back the clock, ushering in "the olden times" (*mukashi* 昔). The art of *manzai*, dating back to ancient China, entered Japan and became "Japanized" in the ninth or tenth century (Groemer 364).

Issa's haiku honors this time-honored tradition of "olden days" and the performers' commitment to preserve it.

In other haiku, he celebrates the comic aspect of *manzai*.

> 万ざいや麦にも一つ祝ひ捨 (1811; *IZ* 1.47)
> *manzai ya mugi ni mo hitotsu iwai sute*
>
> begging actors—
> even the wheat field
> gets a song
>
> 万歳や馬の尻へも一祝 (1812; *IZ* 1.47)
> *manzai ya uma no shiri e mo hito iwai*
>
> begging actors—
> even the horse's rump
> gets a song

The enthusiastic singers go beyond their normal duty of blessing the home, devoting songs to, and thus bestowing luck upon, a farmer's field of *mugi* 麦, a generic term for wheat, barley, oats, or rye. And even the rump of a horse receives a New Year's incantation, thus theoretically securing for the beast ten thousand years of good fortune.

The female counterparts to begging actors were Twelfth Month singers, women who also traveled from town to town, blessing homes with their lucky incantations. In the last ten days or so of the year, Twelfth Month singers, wearing big straw hats decorated with good-luck ferns and with their mouths and noses covered by red or white scarves, sang end-of-year blessings, keeping time by beating on their chests or hitting the ground with drumsticks of split bamboo. Like the *manzai*, the Twelfth Month singers (*sekkizōrō*, sometimes shortened to *sekizoro*) practiced an ancient art with religious overtones, the partially hidden faces of the women hinting of a shamanistic past when masked holy women from the forest may have descended from their mountain retreats to bless the people living in villages below. Whereas the *manzai* were invited into the houses, Twelfth Month singers stood outside, singing until someone from the home would emerge to offer them coins or rice. Their standard song wished riches for home owners much like those of the *manzai* "wit."

> T'is the end of the season!
> As in every year, in every year,
> may the treasures, silver and gold
> gather and fly to the storehouse
> of this honorable home owner! (Greve)

Some of Issa's haiku about Twelfth Month singers sound like praise-songs.

> おく小野や藪もせき候節季候 (? ; *IZ* 1.670)
> *oku ono ya yabu mo sekizoro sekkizoro*
>
> remote field—
> even in a thicket
> Twelfth Month singers!
>
> せき候よ女せき候それも御代 (1813; *IZ* 1.670)
> *sekizoro yo onna sekizoro sore mo miyo*
>
> the Twelfth Month singers
> are female . . .
> our Great Age!

In the first haiku Issa seems proud to be living in a land where end-of-year good luck singers are performing their quasi-religious songs literally everywhere, even in the most remote, backwoods areas—blessing a humble home nestled deep in the trees. The second haiku also exudes a patriotic pride for these traveling woman singers, declaring that their existence "too" (*mo*) contributes to *miyo* 御代: the emperor's reign and the prosperity of the coming new imperial year. Despite their poverty and near-beggar status, these street performers are obviously, deeply, appreciated by Issa.

In another poem Issa's tone is comical.

せき候の尻の先也角田川　(1818; *IZ* 1.671)
sekizoro no shiri no saki nari sumida-gawa

Twelfth Month singers—
their butts facing
Sumida River

In the early 1800s Issa rented a house in Katsushika, an area of land just east of Edo, across Sumida River. This haiku of 1818, written when Issa was living once again in his home province of Shinano, could either be a memory piece or a work of imagination. In it, the Twelfth Month singers perform their incantations while facing a house. Bending low to pound their drumsticks of bamboo or other percussion instruments against the ground, their derrières, Issa humorously notices, all rise and point in unison at the river behind them. Their song wishing good fortune juxtaposes interestingly with the great, flowing river behind them, inviting readers to meditate on possible implications buried within the comedy of the moment. For example, one might reflect upon the ancientness of the river: how it might embody the ancientness of *sekizoro* art. Or, if one considers water a symbol for life, Sumida River might figuratively emphasize the singers' wishes for the prosperity and health of the people of the home. The river, like time, flows on, but in this precious present moment a group of chest-beating spiritual women bring past and future together with an ancient song of good wishes for the coming year. All in all, the haiku is a happy, deeply appreciative portrait of the Twelfth Month singers.

Also happy is a haiku written the following year, in which Issa underscores the revelry inspired by the Twelfth Month singers' annual visit.

子の真似を親もする也せつきぞろ (1819; *IZ* 1.671)
ko no mane wo oya mo suru nari sekkizoro

parents acting
like little kids . . .
Twelfth Month singers!

The haiku is reminiscent of Issa's hokku of 1797, discussed in Chapter 1, in which he expresses his desire to become a child again on New Year's Day. Here, the adults in the scene are doing something like that by literally "imitating the children" (*ko no mane* 子の真似). The holiday singers serve as a catalyst for a moment of joyful rejuvenation in a scene that reminds readers that a new year, new spring, is just about to begin. Readers, too, can become young again—at least, young at heart—by imagining the moment and placing themselves vicariously in it. Issa's respect for the moving power of music and song is, again, palpable.

The most famous female entertainers of Issa's time were, of course, the geisha. Unlike the wandering Twelfth Month singers, who in terms of social class might best be described as talented beggars, the geisha performed their music and dance primarily in the elegantly appointed licensed prostitution quarters, though the majority of them were not prostitutes (Seigle 117). The geisha of the Yoshiwara, Edo's principle pleasure district, earned fame especially as players of the samisen (also called shamisen), a three-stringed banjo-like instrument that came from Japan's southern island of Okinawa. Originally covered with snakeskin, the samisen's sound box on Japan's main islands was covered with cat's skin, and its strings were plucked with a large plectrum. In the following haiku, Issa's mere mention of a samisen conjures, for the reader's imagination, a kimono-clad geisha.

せき候も三弦にのる都哉 (1820; *IZ* 1.671)
sekizoro mo samisen ni noru miyako kana

a samisen joins
the Twelfth Month singers . . .
Kyoto

The setting is Kyoto (*miyako* 都); no longer the center of government and military power (which had shifted to Edo), Kyoto remained the cultural center where the emperor and his court resided. In this city drenched with Japanese history and tradition, a geisha adds her music to that of the roving beggar-singers—a wonderful expression of harmony transcending social classes. In fact, this impromptu concert of Twelfth Month singers and a geisha musician implies their oneness. Whether they wear rags or silk kimonos is immaterial; what matters, Issa seems to suggest, is the pure joy of music.

In another poetic portrait Issa emphasizes, it would seem, a young geisha's filial devotion.

三絃で親やしなふや花の陰 (1821; *IZ* 1.217)
samisen de oya yashinau ya hana no kage

with a samisen
she supports her parents . . .
blossom shade

The scene is possibly unfolding in one of the licensed pleasure districts such as the Yoshiwara. A young geisha performer earns money not for herself but to support her parents. Issa leaves it to the reader's imagination to decide on the poem's emotional tone, which depends on the geisha's background story. Have the girl's parents perhaps sold her to pay their debts (a common practice), in which case she performs her music as an unwilling prisoner in the high-walled, guarded district? Or, has she entered her profession voluntarily, eager to help out her parents in any way that she can? The scene takes place in the shade of blossoms, which in haiku parlance can specifically signify cherry blossoms. Their freshness and fragile beauty serve as an analogue for the young samisen player. However one decides to interpret the girl's situation, Issa sketches her with depth and humanity. Outwardly beautiful, she is even more beautiful in her soul.

In the following haiku about geisha musicians, Issa portrays them putting their instrument and its plectrum to unconventional uses.

> 三弦で雪を降らする二階哉　(1815; *IZ* 1.642)
> *samisen de yuki wo furasuru ni kai kana*
>
> with her samisen
> she makes snow fall . . .
> second floor
>
> 三絃のばちで掃きやる霰哉　(1821; *IZ* 1.649)
> *samisen no bachi de haki yaru arare kana*
>
> with the samisen's
> plectrum sweeping up . . .
> hailstones

The first haiku has the prescript, "Yoshiwara," identifying its location as Edo's prime pleasure district. Although some courtesans played the samisen, the female geisha of Japan became especially proficient at and associated with this instrument, particularly those of the Yoshiwara, who enjoyed a reputation for being dignified artists, unlike the geisha in less refined districts. For example those who worked in Edo's Fukugawa neighborhood often participated in prostitution; in fact, many of the Fukagawa geisha, when arrested for unsanctioned prostitution, were sentenced to years of servitude in the Yoshiwara (Seigle 175). The snow sweeper of the first poem, then, is almost certainly a geisha and not a courtesan. She uses her samisen to clear the snow from a window ledge or balcony, causing an impromptu flurry below. The musician in the second example uses her samisen's plectrum to sweep up hailstones. The close similarity of situation and action in the two haiku suggests that the second is most likely taking place in the same setting as the first, the Yoshiwara, and that the same person is involved: a geisha musician. Although even the geisha of the Yoshiwara could take on lovers and certainly applied their talents to please male clients of the licensed brothels, they were for the most part, to repeat, not prostitutes, and so they managed to achieve, on the basis of their talent alone, "a professional status as entertainers difficult even for men" (174). These matching haiku by Issa capture light, slice-of-life moments in the pleasure district without a hint of outrage at the injustice of women being kept against their wills. Quite the contrary: by engaging in the domestic chore of sweeping—though using unusual "brooms"—the geisha in these scenes seem perfectly at home, perfectly content. As we will learn in the next chapter, Issa's portraits of the Yoshiwara's courtesans are not always as happy or as implicitly approving.

Some of the most accomplished geisha samisen players of the pleasure district became renowned celebrities. The same is true of the top sumo wrestlers in the land, although, as Issa reminds readers in the next haiku, some competitors never attained the status of champion.

> 負角力其子の親も見て居るか (1792; *IZ* 1.506)
> *make-zumō sono ko no oya mo mite iru ka*

defeated sumo wrestler—
is his father
watching too?

Or, Issa's question might be translated, "are his parents/ watching too?" In an undated revision, Issa is more assertive: "his father *must* be watching." A later poem of 1824 might be read in poignant juxtaposition with both versions.

角力になると祝ふ親のこゝろ哉 (1824; *IZ* 1.508)
sumō ni naru to iwau oya no kokoro kana

he's become a
sumo wrestler!
the proud parents

The "hearts" (*kokoro* こゝろ) of the wrestler's parents swell with pride, but after a son's defeat, one can only imagine—as Issa invites us to—an athlete's feeling of disappointment and, perhaps, deep shame. Issa, who suffered his share of setbacks and personal tragedies in life, identified and sympathized with underdogs—and even with under*frogs*, as evidenced by his famous words of encouragement to a skinny frog outmatched during a territorial pond battle: "don't give up!/ Issa is here." His haiku about the defeated wrestler draws sympathetic attention to his emotional suffering, although—like the master haiku poet that he is— Issa manages to convey emotion without overtly emotional adjectives, letting the image speak for itself.

Haiku portraits of sumo champions are just as perceptive and attuned to the humanity and perhaps surprising tenderness of these large athletes.

草花をよけて居るや勝角力 (1807; *IZ* 1.506)
kusabana wo yokete suwaru ya kachi sumō

> avoiding the wildflowers
> he squats . . .
> sumo champion

Issa wrote this haiku in 1807 while visiting a Shinto shrine, Ouchi, during an annual festival that took place from the fourth to fifteenth days of Ninth Month in the old Japanese calendar (*IZ* 2.552). Although sumo wrestling had achieved status as a professional sport by Issa's time, its old medieval roots in Shinto ritual remained evident (as they still are today), with tournaments often taking place on the grounds of Shinto shrines, with officiators dressed in similar fashion as Shinto priests, and with the consecrated circle of combat (*dohyō* 土俵) representing the earth below while its roof represented the heavens above. Sumo wrestling's practical purpose remained as it had for centuries: the solicitation of divine help to ensure a good harvest. In Issa's haiku, a presumably massive champion performing at Ouchi Shrine respectfully avoids squashing wildflowers, indicating that a kind heart beats within his imposing physical frame. In two later poems wrestlers exhibit a similar degree of concern for small, fragile lives.

> 勝角力虫も踏ずにもどりけり (1823; *IZ* 1.508)
> *kachi sumō mushi mo fumazu ni modori keri*
>
> sumo champion—
> he won't even step
> on a bug
>
> 角力取が詫して逃す雀かな (1825; *IZ* 1.509)
> *sumōtori ga wabi shite nogasu suzume kana*

the sumo wrestler
apologizing, releases
the sparrow

Literally, the gentle giant in the haiku of 1823, "walks around a bug (or worm) so as not to step on it." In the related poem of two years later, one of a series of nine haiku in a row on the topic of sumo in Issa's journal (*IZ* 2.554), a wrestler releases a sparrow as part of the Buddhist ceremony of *hōjō-e*: the so-called "merit release" of captive animals. This ritual of compassion originated as a Chinese cultural practice that, with the support of apocryphal sutras, eventually became accepted as a very popular Buddhist rite (Shiu 184). It was performed at times for the wellbeing of the person releasing the animal but also, quite commonly, for the wellbeing of one's family, including one's ancestors in the context of a memorial service. Whatever the precise circumstances that prevail in Issa's poem, the wrester in it shows respect and concern for the small bird, setting it free. Incidentally, we might note in passing that Issa doesn't explore and most likely did not contemplate the ethical dilemma involved in "merit-releases": the fact that often three times the number of animals (birds, turtles, fish) had to be captured to provide temples with an adequate supply of animals to release in these ceremonies. Today, the spread of bird flu and the problems of endangered and invasive species add to the questionable nature of this "compassionate" practice (see Shiu 188).

Issa wrote dozens of haiku on the topic of sumo wrestlers, but perhaps the most poignant is the following.

角力とりやはるばる来る親の塚 (1814; *IZ* 1.507)
sumōtori ya haru-baru kinuru oya no tsuka

> the sumo wrestler
> has come from afar . . .
> parents' grave

Like crossroads singers, begging actors, Twelfth Month singers, and geisha musicians of the pleasure districts; Japan's sumo wrestlers traveled to urban centers from all over the country, leaving parents behind in their native villages. In this haiku, a wrestler's return trip home has been quite long, and it most likely has been a quite long while since he left his parents to pursue a career in professional sumo. Perhaps his village is so remote that he expected to find his parents still alive but instead has discovered—depending on how one interprets *oya no tsuka* 親の塚 —his "parents' burial mound" or "one of his parent's burial mound." Whether he knew in advance of his parents' deaths (or of one parent's death), the wrestler must be emotionally devastated. He has succeed in life, for if he hadn't done well at sumo would he have traveled so far away? Nevertheless, his triumph is hollow. The parents who would have been proud to welcome him home have died without him there to be able to tend to them or even to tell them goodbye. Now, standing at their burial spot for their ashes (or, the reader might choose to imagine the single grave containing the ashes of a dear mother or father), the wrestler's heart, we can assume, is breaking. As usual, Issa plumbs the emotional depths of a human heart without emotional descriptors, relying on his image alone and the imaginations of his readers.

The talented performers depicted in the haiku of Issa endure poverty, hard weather, hard travel, and separation from their loved ones to bring moments of entertainment and beauty to their public in the form of a lucky incantations, irreverent jokes, exquisite music, and astounding feats of athleticism. As a master haiku poet who understood perfectly the capaciousness of understatement, Issa manages to suggest rather than outright explain the dedication and humanity of these artists. He shows them in moments of dejection and elation, with a strong subtext of pride running through their poetic portraits: the pride of performers who sacrifice much for their art and for their families. And also palpable as subtext is Issa's own pride in the ability of entertainers to preserve and to add to the time-honored artistic traditions of Japan, thereby bringing back, if only for wondrous and fleeting moments, the "olden times."

Chapter 7. PROSTITUTES

In his haiku portraits of the neglected and downtrodden, Issa exhibited a deep and lively compassion that became forever associated with his name. He considered beggars, peasants, orphans, and even (as we shall see in the next chapter) ethnic minority outcastes, the Ainu, to be worthy subjects in his one-breath sketches: not looked down upon but rather appreciated as human beings who love and need love, who get drunk on nature's beauty, and who stoically endure harsh weather, rapacious taxation, and the cruelty of stepmothers. Accordingly, Issa's first critics in Japan, two admirers who penned the postscripts for the posthumous publication of his prose-and-haiku journal *Oraga haru* in 1852, understandably singled out "human feeling" (*ninjō*) as a hallmark of his poetic style.[40] Did Issa's famous human feeling extend as well to the socially oppressed women of Tokugawa society? As a male poet acculturated in the male-dominant Japan of his era, did Issa's penetrating sympathy for fellow creatures, from insects to Ainu, extend also to the economically, socially, and—in some cases—physically enslaved women of his time? An examination of his haiku about prostitutes—from the highest class courtesans of the Yoshiwara down to the lowest grade of streetwalker—will help answer these questions.

He wrote the following haiku in one of his notebooks with the head note, "Brothel Music."

三弦のばちでうけたり雪礫　(1814; *IZ* 1.696)
samisen no bachi de uketari yukitsubute

blocked with her
samisen's plectrum . . .
snowball

A skillfully written haiku such as this one leaves much to the reader's imagination. Has the snowball been thrown by a rowdy, possibly drunk customer, or perhaps by a courtesan? Whoever has thrown the snowball, the samisen player (most likely a geisha musician) cleverly fends off the attack. The presence of a samisen indicates that the brothel is elegant and high-class, suggesting that the scene is taking place in a licensed pleasure district, quite possibly the Yoshiwara on the outskirts of Edo. A five-block area surrounded by a moat on three sides with a guarded gate on the fourth, the Yoshiwara confined between two and three thousand courtesans (Sone 171). Like *ukiyo-e* artists of the period who painted scenes of the sumptuous "Floating World" of such districts and their renowned courtesans, Issa focuses his (and our) attention on a light-hearted moment: a snowball attack on (as I choose to picture it) the brothel's verandah, causing a resourceful samisen player to defend herself with her plectrum. This playful image could fittingly grace a painting of the era, such as those done by Harunobu (1724-1770) for his color printed book, *A Comparison of Beauties of the Green Houses*, each one including a haiku by Kasaya Saren.[41] Sexual tourism was encouraged by such popular guides to the licensed pleasure quarters, in which high-class courtesans appeared as the glamorous pop stars of their time. However, despite their posh rooms, extravagant kimonos, and at times possibly authentic feelings of love for their rich customers, "life for the courtesan was mainly an unpleasant form of female slavery" (Illing, "Introduction"). Amy Stanley adds that prostitution during Japan's early modern period involved "the subjugation of women during a period of intense social repression" (1). Though they were idealized in art and publications—and featured as heroines in stories and kabuki plays—Edo-period sex workers rarely enjoyed the proceeds from their labor, unlike their parents, kidnappers, or whoever initially sold them. Issa, however, offers no hint of this disturbing truth underlying his happy scene of flying snowballs at a brothel.

In an early poem written when Issa was thirty he praises courtesans and their talents, and, once again, disappointingly provides no evidence that the sympathy that he expressed so often for fleas and flies extended as well to the female human beings who made their living by selling sex and the illusion of love.

能い女郎衆岡崎女郎衆夕涼み (1792; *IZ* 1.318)
yoi joroshu okazaki joroshu yūsuzumi

skillful courtesans!
Okazaki courtesans!
enjoying evening's cool

On the 25th day of Third Month that year, Issa set off on a journey to the southern island of Shikoku, recording his haiku impressions in *Kansei kuchō* ("Kansei Era Verse Collection"). In this poem from that collection, he praises the *jorō* 女郎 of the licensed pleasure district in Okazaki, one of the fifty-three post towns on the Tōkaidō highway from Edo to Kyoto. *Jorō* can refer to a geisha or prostitute.[42] In the scene, they sit outside on a summer evening, presumably on the veranda of their brothel, enjoying the coolness. Issa gives no indication that though the cool air moves freely, the women cannot; that they are prisoners confined by a tall palisade that completely surrounds the quarter, its single gate well-guarded by an armed *yoriki* (feudal policeman; Nouet 91). Once again Issa's portrait of life in a brothel reads like a commercial for it, making him appear as just another male chauvinist of his period, objectifying female sex workers without a hint of a deeper understanding or sympathy.

However, in other haiku Issa goes deeper, psychologically. The following undated one, for example, depicts a high-ranking courtesan interacting with a child.

傾城がかはいがりけり小せき候 (?; *IZ* 1.672)
keisei ga kawaigari keri ko sekizoro

the beautiful courtesan
pets the child . . .
Twelfth Month singer

The setting is a pleasure district in winter. Twelfth Month singers, who have been wandering from town to town singing festive songs for tips, perform their act at a brothel. Based on external appearances, the courtesan in the scene, whom we can visualize as painstakingly coiffed and dressed in a fine kimono, seems to belong to a different planet than the poor, ragged minstrels, whose faces are covered (according to custom) by scarves. The woman reaches out a hand to caress one child singer, a little girl—and this is all that Issa presents on the literal level. However, as a haiku this verse is far superior to the previous examples, for it evokes a world of meaning and emotion beneath the surface of its words. As a prisoner within the walled enclave of the pleasure district, the courtesan's profession is to provide entertainment and sex to customers in a fantasy world of costume, music, drinking, dance, flirtation, and poetry. While she might give (or might have already given) birth at a secret maternity hospital, she is not allowed to play the role of mother beyond that. In fact, in the case of pregnancy a courtesan in a licensed pleasure district would more likely be forced to take an abortion-inducing drug than to carry a child to term because, as one scholar of early modern Japan puts it, "prostitution as an institution denied maternity" (Sone 179). Issa leaves to the reader's imagination to question the depths of what this courtesan may be feeling while caressing the minstrel child—regret, longing, desperate sadness, or simply a numb awareness of what can never be? And since the child, like all Twelfth Month singers, is female, might the indentured prostitute perhaps identify with her, glimpsing her own past in the little girl's poverty and lack of choice in the oppressive world of Tokugawa Japan where "daughter selling" to relieve a family's debt was sadly common (Stanley 113)?

In other haiku, Issa directs our attention to young courtesans, as in this example from 1810.

菜の花や袖を苦にする小傾城 (1810; *IZ* 1.186)
na no hana ya sode wo ku ni suru ko keisei

flowering mustard—
the young courtesan
worries about her sleeves

Ko keisei 小傾城 can mean "little beauty," "little courtesan," or "little prostitute." The girl is most likely a courtesan in training because she "worries about her sleeves," fearing that the flowers of the mustard plant (also referred to as rape and canola) will stain them with their golden dust. Novice courtesans by custom wore long-sleeved kimonos, so the girl in the scene, if she is wearing such a garment, would have reason to gather up and attempt to protect her sleeves from the flowers. On the surface, the haiku simply captures a slice-of-life moment, but the image of innocent beauty alongside potentially staining flowers (due to the yellow pollen that contains the plant's male gametes, i.e. its sperm cells) creates a sexually charged symbolism. The young girl in the scene might manage to preserve the purity of her kimono, but not, ultimately, her virginity, which will be sold to the highest bidder. By showing a child preoccupied with keeping untarnished the sleeves of her new uniform for sexual labor, Issa hints of the underlying, pathetic truth of her existence.

In a later haiku about a young courtesan, Issa again evokes sympathy through the skillful manipulation of imagery.

>霜がれや鍋の炭かく小傾城 (1821; *IZ* 1.735)
>*shimogare ya nabe no sumi kaku ko keisei*
>
>frost-killed grass—
>the young courtesan
>scrapes soot from a kettle

In this poem Issa again uses the ambiguous phrase, *ko keisei*, which may be read as referring to a "little beauty" or to a novice courtesan. I agree with Makoto Ueda, who opts for the less innocent reading in his translation of this haiku (137). Issa's image of "frost-killed grass" (*shimogare* 霜がれ) suggests the idea of innocence cut short, of youth destroyed, of a premature winter in the seasonal round of Life's Year—making the translation of *keisei* as courtesan seem practically necessary. Instead of a romanticized and objectified portrait of elegance, Issa presents here a young prostitute engaged in cold, menial labor: scraping soot from a kettle. Without including a word that would directly describe an emotion, his simple juxtaposition of the images of frost-killed grass with a girl's dreary winter chore make Issa's sympathy, though unspoken, evident.

This next haiku portrays a courtesan at the other end of her career. After what we might assume to be many years of work in a pleasure district, she finally returns to her native village and bestows a special gift upon a statue of Amida Buddha.

>傾城や在所のみだへ衣配 (1825; *IZ* 1.678)
>*keisei ya zaisho no mida e kinu kubari*

> beautiful courtesan—
> new clothes for her hometown's
> Buddha

Another winter poem, the haiku alludes to the Twelfth Month custom of providing gifts of new clothes, usually for one's relatives. Here, the courtesan returns to her provincial hometown, piously offering such a gift to Amida Buddha. According to Shinran, the founder of the Jōdoshinshū sect of Pure Land Buddhism to which Issa and the majority of Japanese in his time belonged, even great sinners can be reborn in the Western Paradise or Pure Land, if they rely utterly on the Other Power of Amida. Issa could have therefore expected his original readers to understand the courtesan's gesture as a powerful acknowledgement of Amida's Original Vow to rescue all beings who sincerely trust in his power. In this scene there is no glamorizing or objectifying of the sex worker. Instead, she appears simply as a human being who, like all humans, is flawed and unworthy by her own efforts to attain the Pure Land and enlightenment, but who—also like all others—can pray to and trust in the Beyond.

This remarkable haiku invites further reflection. The fact that the beautiful prostitute presents clothes to Amida and not to a living relative—parent or child—emphasizes the solitude required of her social role. She seems utterly alone in this portrait: without a parent to whom she might offer filial devotion, without a child whom she might clothe and coddle. Instead, she goes to a public space for worship and offers her gift to a lifeless statue. Issa's mastery of understatement, adroitly expressing ideas more by what he leaves out than by what he puts in, is impressive in this haiku.

Based on examples thus far, one might derive the impression that Issa's compassionate understanding of prostitutes grew with time, from his simplistic praising of the "skillful courtesans" of Okazaki in 1792 to his more emotionally complex vision in 1825 of a courtesan offering new clothes to Amida Buddha. This impression is not accurate. In a poem that appeared, like his "skillful courtesans" verse, in *Kansei kuchō*—this one written during the second year of his journey (1793)—Issa reveals that even in his early poetry he was capable of deeply heartfelt portraiture of female sex workers.

さらぬだに月に立待惣稼哉 (1793; *IZ* 1.462)
saranu dani tsuki ni tachimatsu sōka kana

not only waiting
for the harvest moon to rise . . .
streetwalker

The streetwalker in the scene, a *sōka* 惣稼, was the lowest grade of prostitute who worked the roadsides in Issa's time (*IZ* 2.60). The woman in the scene isn't only waiting for the splendor of the moon; she's waiting for customers, too, to "rise"—that is, to appear and, quite possibly, in the sexual connotation of the verb, to have erections. The *tachimatsu* moon is that of the 17th day of Eighth Month—two days past the full harvest moon. It's still brilliant but already waning, perhaps imbuing the scene, for some readers, with a sense of missed opportunity and a subtle feeling of regret. In his book, *Issa to onnatachi* ("Issa and Women"), Kobayashi Masafumi cites this poem as an example of a haiku that "strikes the heart" (41). As with the much-later written haiku about the courtesan presenting clothes to Amida, this early poem suggests the prostitute's isolation. She waits in darkness for the moon, for a man, for subsistence. While poets can afford to wait for moonrise as a pretext to make a haiku, the streetwalker has less lofty, more mundane and pressing concerns. The moon will light the way for the men who will arrive that night and "also rise." Even with its hint of low humor the poem is filled with a sense of pathos: a sympathetic, clear-eyed, and certainly unromanticized view of a street prostitute's existence.

In a later haiku Issa again associates women of the evening with a darkness—both physical and metaphorical.

> 夜に入れば遊女袖引く柳哉　(1823; *IZ* 1.241)
> *yo ni ireba yūjo sode hiku yanagi kana*

> when night falls
> whores tug at sleeves . . .
> willow tree

Or, this haiku might be translated to evoke a single prostitute tugging at a man's sleeves. A spring season word, willow trees suggest freshness and new life with the sprouting of their delicate, shade-providing leaves. They are also associated with, and therefore connote, red-light districts. The expression, *sode hiku* 袖引く, literally denotes dragging one by the sleeve, but symbolically suggests seduction. When night falls, seduction begins: men are "pulled" not only physically by the prostitutes but also by their own sexual urges, so acute in springtime. Again, Issa places poetic emphasis on the aloneness of the women: shadowy figures lurking in darkness, reaching out to pull men, both physically and symbolically, toward them and away from light.

In a similar haiku written a year later, in 1824, Issa again links a streetwalker with darkness.

> かはほりや夜ほちの耳の辺りより (1824; *IZ* 1.335)
> *kawahori ya yahochi no mimi no atari yori*

> a bat—
> buzzing the ear
> of the hooker

The Japanese word for wife, *kanai* 家内, means "in the house." In stark contrast, the streetwalkers of the Edo period, as Stanley notes, were "literally women outside the household" (7). At a time in which womanly virtues included "obedience, chastity, mercy, and quietness"—as listed in a popular guide for girls' instruction—streetwalkers represented a brazen antithesis to the socially accepted norm (Ekken 23). Due to the lack of a welfare system for the poor, many public authorities chose to look the other way, and some even accepted the notion that unauthorized prostitution "benefited society" (Sone 183). Nevertheless, the woman depicted in this haiku example belongs to the class of prostitute that convinced many samurai officials that their anti-domestic behavior was dangerously "destabilizing the realm" (Stanley 10).

Yahochi is another word for *yotaka*—"nighthawk." Both words in Issa's time were euphemisms for low-grade streetwalkers who waited for customers on roadsides in the evening.[43] Such women, many of whom suffered from the final stages of syphilis, aggressively overturned the Japanese ideal of feminine modesty and reticence, "pounc[ing] on men after dark" (Sone 178; Stanely 14). They worked under cover of darkness not only because underground prostitution was illegal and carried heavy fines (a three-year sentence in the Yoshiwara) but because some of the syphilitic ones lacked complete noses, heads of hair, and suffered from curved spines (Sone 178; 182). This is a dark poem, indeed: nighttime, night "bird" (the woman), and a night-flying bat that whisks past, seemingly emanating from the prostitute's ear. The mood, too, is dark, despite Issa's somewhat playful suggestion that these two beings who fly by night are kindred spirits. Issa's deeper feelings about the situation are unstated; he allows the minimalistic scene of a bat flying from a night hawk's (prostitute's) ear to speak for itself, and in so doing eloquently suggests empathy for the solitary survival quests of two creatures of darkness.

In this next haiku, Issa again portrays a lower class of prostitute than those found in Japan's elegant brothels. This time the scene unfolds in broad daylight.

遊女めが見てけっかるぞ暑い舟 (1817; *IZ* 1.250)
yūjome ga mite kekkaru zo atsui fune

the whores
look me over . . .
from their boat in the heat

Another possible reading of this haiku would be: "the whore/ looks me over . . . / from her boat in the heat." In his commentary on this poem Jean Cholley notes that prostitutes operated on boats on the west bank of Sumida River in Edo. Their price was 32 *mon,* which in Issa's day would buy about three bowls of rice (243). As with all excellent haiku, the poem consists of a seemingly objective presentation of images: prostitutes (or a single prostitute) on a boat on a hot summer day, looking at something or someone. This action is conveyed with the words *mite kekkaru* 見てけっかる; literally, they "are looking" (or she "is looking"). The object of the gaze is unstated but strongly implied: the poet, a potential customer. Also strongly implied is the fact that this looking will be in vain. The scene is static: little movement, no excitement, no hope for success in the oppressive heat. The prostitutes look but do not call out or beckon; perhaps they have instantly appraised the poet's poor clothing and have decided that there's little chance to do business with him. Issa might even be injecting a bit of dry humor in the scene: even the minimal effort of looking at him, "Shinano Province's Chief Beggar," is a waste of the prostitutes' time and energy. After the seemingly eternal moment depicted in the poem, one can imagine Issa continuing his journey and the prostitutes continuing their long, hard wait under the sun. Once again, without the use of emotional words in the poem, the emotion of compassion is triggered in the hearts and minds of Issa's readers.

In a final example of a haiku portrait of a low-grade prostitute, Issa's compassion is again unspoken but strongly suggested.

> 木がらしや二十四文の遊女小家 (1819; *IZ* 632)
> *kogarashi ya ni jūshi mon no yūjo-goya*
>
> winter wind—
> a twenty-four penny
> whorehouse

In Issa's day twenty-four copper *mon* coins were sufficient to purchase approximately two bowls of rice or three servings of low-quality sushi. In contrast to this paltry amount, a night with a prostitute in Edo and its vicinity could run as high as one thousand *mon*, and in provincial post-town brothels, customers expected to pay between three hundred and five hundred *mon* (Stanley xxii). In terms of contemporary currency, Issa is therefore depicting in this poem something akin to a "ten-dollar whorehouse": the lowest of the low in terms of prostitution under a roof. The woman or women in the "little house" (*goya* 小家) sells her body (or their bodies) at a bargain basement price to survive in a cold and indifferent world. As Sone points out, most of the unsanctioned houses of prostitution were "extremely small in scale, employing only one or two women" who were sometimes coerced and managed by poverty-stricken husbands (177). Others were seduced or raped by the owner of the business and were constantly watched by enforcers, making their escape as near to impossible as it was for the high-class courtesans of Edo's Yoshiwara, Osaka's Shin-machi, or Kyoto's Shimabara districts (177). As with the heat in the previous example and the darkness in the one before that, the natural context helps establish the poem's mood. In this case, the mood is desperate: instead of customers, winter is arriving at the prostitute's hovel in the form of a bitter-cold wind, raising the question: How will the woman (or women) within survive? Once again, Issa presents images without guiding his readers' response to them, yet the reader who senses pathos and human concern in the scene is likely feeling as Issa felt, for they have been skillfully directed to this emotion by the poet's words and omissions.

The reference to lowly *yūjo* 遊女 in this and other haiku would have brought to mind for Issa and many of his contemporary readers a famous poem by his great predecessor, Bashō, recorded in that poet's travel journal, *Oku no hosomichi*.

一家に遊女も寝たり萩と月 (1689; Bashō 1.287)
hitotsu ie ni yūjo mo netari hagi to tsuki

in one house
whores sleep too . . .
bush clover and moon

Bashō's poetic depiction of a night spent in an inn near the barrier gate of Ichiburi presents metaphorically loaded imagery in its concluding phrase, "bush clover and the moon." The prostitutes align symbolically with the flowers in the inn's garden and, by implication, Bashō aligns himself with the moon: distant and serene, shining clearly in the night sky above—suggesting that although he may exist physically in the sublunary world of inns frequented by low-grade prostitutes, spiritually he soars above the scene. Bashō does not condemn the prostitutes, though he alludes to their "sinfulness" in the prose passage that precedes the haiku. He writes of these two travelers from Niigata in the following way: "Their life was such that they had to drift along even as the white froth of waters that beat the shore [. . .] forced to find a new companion each night, they had to renew their pledge of love at every turn, thus proving each time the fatal sinfulness of their nature" (Matsuo Bashō, *The Narrow Road* 131). In the haiku that follows shortly after these comments, Bashō pays the prostitutes a sort of compliment, suggesting a comparison between them and the blooming flowers. However, the resulting poem is one of aesthetic distancing between the priest-like poet ("moon") and the worldly working women ("bush clover"), who sleep near enough to him that he can hear them talking through a thin wall. Though the prose passage that introduces the haiku contains words of compassion, this emotion is not suggested in the poem itself. Issa, on the other hand, presents a perhaps conscious difference between himself and his poetic role model. Instead of hollowly complimenting (hence objectifying) a prostitute for her physical attractiveness, he hides her, unseen, in a poor shack battered by a frigid wind. Instead of the aesthetic aloofness of Bashō, we find in this haiku, and in previous examples, the big-hearted sympathy of Issa.

In the following haiku, the first one that Issa recorded in his journal, *Shichiban nikki*, for Second Month, 1817; prostitution isn't overtly mentioned but, to some Japanese critics, it is implied.

> 笠でするさらばさらばや薄がすみ (1817; *IZ* 1.86)
> *kasa de suru saraba saraba ya usu-gasumi*

> waving umbrella-hats
> farewell! farewell!
> thin mist

Issa prefaces the poem with "Spring colors at Karuizawa"—a historic town in his home province of Shinano, today's Nagano Prefecture. In it, he evokes a scene of two people bidding one another farewell in spring mist. Because of the mist, their hand gestures and bowing heads are hard to see. As one walks away from the other, his or her shape is soon swallowed by the mist, and is seen no more. Issa captures the delicate emotion that the Japanese call *sabi* 寂び—a sort of existential loneliness that Bashō valued highly in haiku. Japanese critic Kobayashi Masafumi believes that the scene depicts two lovers parting in the morning, more specifically, a man (possibly Issa) and his *ichiyazuma* 一夜妻 ("one-night wife"), a prostitute (44). An Edo maxim of the period asserted, "The standard lie of the prostitute is 'I love you'; the standard lie of the client is, 'I will marry you'" (Seigle 189). Contemporary books for courtesans recommended that they fake emotions in the presence of clients, especially when parting, shedding tears and assuming "an air of grief" (190). Nevertheless, the engendering of genuine and deep bonds of emotional attachment between prostitute and customer was quite common, reflected in the high number of double suicides (*aitaijini* 相対死) involving a man and a prostitute who—because they were forbidden to wed in this life, decided to die together in hopes of a future-life marriage (179-80). If one interprets the partner in Issa's poem to be a prostitute, she may not be one of high rank (or she may be disguised), since she waves a *kasa* 笠: the broad, rustic headgear of peasants. Whatever her status, the fact that the two are waving goodbye hints at a feeling of shared warmth and genuine affection, an emotionally important connection, perhaps. Nevertheless, their night of passion and sex-trade (if Kobayashi Masafumi is correct in his interpretation of the scene) is now over, and the two go their separate ways, vanishing into morning mist. The love of a one-night wife, Issa suggests, is ephemeral and yet, maybe, tender and sincere.

A haiku of 1794 more plainly draws a connection between morning mist and a separation of lovers.

きぬぎぬやかすむ迄見る妹が家 (1794; *IZ* 1.82)
kinu-ginuyaka sumu made miru imo ga ie

lovers parting—
looking back at her house
until only mist

Issa prefaces this haiku with the phrase, "Parting lovers," and ends it with the words, *imo ga ie* 妹が家, which literally translate as "dear one's house," *imo* being an intimate term that a man uses to refer to his beloved.[44] According to Makoto Ueda, this early poem represents an attempt at Tenmei style, a school of haiku that valued aestheticism and fictional elegance (31). A man, possibly Issa, walks away from his lover's house, looking back at it again and again until, finally, it fades into the mist. If one chooses to read this early haiku as well as the later one about the waving umbrella-hats as depictions of the parting of lovers, one of whom may have been paid for the tryst, they are surprisingly tender treatments of such a situation.

Some of Issa's poetic depictions of Tokugawa era prostitutes suggest his admiration of their beauty, their skills, their playfulness. In many others, however, he coaxes readers toward deeper understanding and compassion. He presents the emotionally evocative image of a courtesan, herself not allowed to raise children, tenderly petting the head of a child minstrel. He shows a courtesan in training worried about the potentially symbolic male stain of mustard blossom pollen. He poetically equates, pathetically, another young courtesan with "frost-killed grass," and he presents a presumably older one as a homecoming penitent, alone in the world, offering clothing to Amida Buddha. Lower down the social hierarchy, he juxtaposes streetwalkers and other common prostitutes with images of loneliness, coldness, and darkness—both physical and spiritual. And in some "morning after" haiku in which the presence of prostitutes is hinted at though not overtly stated, he implies that genuine feelings of affection, if not love, may have developed, leading to genuine sorrow in separation. In sum, Issa portrays prostitutes as people more than sex objects: born into and bound by the restrictions of an oppressive, often sordid social world. Like millions of fellow members belonging to the vast class of the downtrodden in that world, these women do what they must to survive. They dream, they regret, they love, they suffer, they wait . . . and some of them—like the beautiful courtesan returning to her hometown to clothe a statue—bow their heads in supplication and surrender to a higher power, hoping for something better.

Chapter 8. BEGGARS, OUTCASTES, THIEVES

As has been mentioned, Issa described himself as "Shinano Province's Chief Beggar" (*Shinano-guni kojiki shūryo Issa*; 信濃国乞食首領一茶), an appellation that might be taken to mean, simply, "poet," since from the outset of his writing career Issa associated the life of wandering haiku poets with that of beggars. In Third Month of 1791, at age twenty-nine, he started out on his first haiku-writing walking tour, a setting-forth that he pointedlyly described as entering "a beggar's world."

雉鳴て梅に乞食の世也けり (1791; *IZ* 1.146)
kiji naite ume ni kojiki no yo nari keri

pheasant crying—
it's a plum blossom-filled
beggar's world now!

The haiku commemorates the beginning of a journey in which Issa planned to emulate Bashō and other wandering poet-monks of Japanese history, begging for his food along the way. Entering the "beggar's world" meant entering the life of a haiku poet and teacher. As his poetic career developed, Issa eventually had scores of *haikai* students scattered throughout Shinano Province whom he would visit often and upon whose generosity and hospitality he relied. In a very real sense, the traveling poet Issa had much in common with beggars, especially homeless ones.

Technically, beggars were considered *hinin* 非人—literally, "nonhuman"—existing outside of the officially recognized social hierarchy of samurai, farmer, artisan, and merchant (prostitutes, discussed in the previous chapter, and thieves, discussed later in this one, also belonged to this *hinin* category; Deal 114). Nevertheless, in one memorable haiku, Issa implies that he and a beggar are virtually indistinguishable.

秋の風乞食は我を見くらぶる (1804; *IZ* 1.467)
aki no kaze kojiki wa ware wo mikuraburu

autumn wind—
a beggar looking
sizes me up

Issa isn't a dispassionate, objective observer. He writes himself into his poetry and interacts with others—people, animals, plants—so much so that some readers can mistake his haiku for mere autobiography. In fact, although his identity as a beggar may have some factual basis—especially in his early years—Issa exaggerates this identity for the sake of poetry, creating the literary persona of a poor, hungry, wandering and downtrodden Everyman. In this interesting poem, a beggar looks at "beggar" Issa with a critical eye and (the reader might assume) decides not to bother asking him for alms. There is humor built into the situation, but the scene has dark implications as well. The chilly autumn wind reminds one that there is nothing funny about hunger and homelessness, especially with winter approaching. Structurally, the poem resembles Issa's widely known verse about a staring contest with a frog.[45] In that haiku of 1819, the image of a frog staring at the poet staring at the frog is also comic with a deeper level of interpretation, for it implies radical equality between Issa and the frog. In similar fashion, the image of a beggar looking at Issa looking back at the beggar suggests, beneath its humor, that Issa and the beggar are fundamentally, at their core, the same.

In other haiku Issa alludes to his own poverty with a more comic tone, as in these examples.

> 正夢や春早々の貧乏神 (1811; *IZ* 1.42)
> *masayume ya haru haya-baya no bimbō-gami*
>
> my dream comes true—
> this spring my god
> the god of the poor
>
> 我宿の貧乏神も御供せよ (1820; *IZ* 1.655)
> *waga yado no bimbō-gami mo o-tomo seyo*
>
> the dirt-poor god
> of my house, too
> joins the throng

The first poem refers to the first dream of the new year, believed to be oracular. In Issa's case, he has dreamed about Bimbōgami, the god of poverty, and so when he wakes to find himself still poor, he jokingly declares that his "dream came true" (*masayume* 正夢). The second poem also humorously references Bimbōgami. The seasonal context is the first month of winter in the old Japanese calendar, Tenth Month, at which time the Shinto gods all depart from their home shrines to congregate at the Izumo-Taisha Shrine. Issa sardonically notes that his own household god, the god of poverty, has joined the throng of the departing divine pilgrims.

Though he on occasion exaggerates his poverty for comic effect, Issa often describes the severe poverty of others with compassion and cognizance of the gravity of their situations.

> 鳥も巣を作るに橋の乞食哉 (1793; *IZ* 1.125)
> *tori mosu wo tsukuru ni hashi no kojiki kana*

even birds
make their nests . . .
beggars under the bridge

はつ雪や朝夷する門乞食 (1810; *IZ* 1.635)
hatsu yuki ya asaebisu suru kado kojiki

first snowfall—
early morning at my gate
a beggar

時雨るや親椀たたく唖乞食 (1819; *IZ* 1.627)
shigururu ya oyawan tataku oshikojiki

winter rain—
the deaf and dumb beggar beats
his bowl

重箱の銭四五文や夕時雨 (1819; *IZ* 1.628)
jūbako no zeni shi go mon ya yūshigure

in the box
four or five *mon* . . .
night of winter rain

These four one-breath poems, read one after the other, create a brilliant and nuanced tableau of beggar life in early modern Japan. In the first, an early haiku of 1793, Issa observes (with a sigh, one imagines) that even birds make cozy homes for themselves, but these huddled-together human beings must sleep under a bridge. In the second poem Issa doesn't explicitly identify the gate as his own, but this might be inferred. Snow is falling, and in the cold dawn a beggar, of necessity, is already waiting at the poet's gate, his hand outstretched in quiet desperation. The third poem, which presents a deaf and dumb beggar beating his bowl in a cold winter rain—making a sound of supplication that he himself cannot hear—is perhaps Issa's quintessential image of poverty, destitution, and human waste at a time when some fellow citizens lived not so very far away in luxury. In his translation of this haiku, William J. Higginson begins simply with the word, "drizzling."[46] However, the fact that Issa begins his original text with a specifically identified *winter* rain (*shigururu* 時雨る) makes the beggar's condition seem even more pitiful: not only is he being soaked in rain; that rain is cold to the bone. In the fourth poem, written that same year, Issa again accentuates the silent suffering of a beggar by setting the scene on a raining winter's day. In one journal he prefaces it with the note, "A temple courtyard beggar." When he recopies it into another journal, *Oraga haru*, he expands the preface to read, "Taking pity on a courtyard beggar at Zenkōji's gate." As noted in an earlier chapter, a bowl of rice cost twelve copper *mon* coins in Issa's time. The amount in the beggar's box, four or five *mon*, is measly, indeed—insufficient even for the poorest of meals. Meanwhile, the winter rain pours down pitilessly into the beggar's box, submerging all of his paltry wealth . . . another image of absolute hopelessness, absolute destitution, in "Great Japan."

Given Issa's identification with and empathy for beggars, it may come as no surprise that he vicariously rejoices in a beggar's small victory on New Year's Day.

乞食やもらひながらのはつ笑ひ (1823; *IZ* 1.42)
kojiki ya morai nagara no hatsu warai

a beggar receives
alms, the year's first
laughter

Many poor people learn to live in and for the present moment, enjoying whatever small pleasures that come their way, because to focus on the future means focusing on just misery and hardship. Interestingly, this haiku of First Month 1823 appears in Issa's *Hachiban nikki* immediately after a poem about a nursing infant.

片乳を握りながらやはつ笑ひ (1823; *IZ* 1.42)
kata chichi wo nigiri nagara ya hatsu warai

while grasping
mama's breast . . .
the year's first laughter

By writing these haiku back-to-back, Issa might subtly be suggesting that the beggar's happy outburst is as spontaneous and pure as a baby's delight. As noted in Chapter 1, a person who can live in the moment like a child—without concern about life's next moment—makes a better candidate for Buddhist enlightenment than well-off individuals whose minds dwell incessantly on future gains or losses. The spontaneous New Year's laughter of this nameless beggar might therefore be interpreted as manifesting an enlightened, present-in-the-moment, spiritual attitude.

Issa returns to the theme of poor folk enjoying and thriving in present moments of luck or beauty despite their poverty in many poems, such as in the following haiku about New Year's kite-flying.

今様の凧上りけり乞食小屋 (1811; *IZ* 1.45)
ima yō no tako agari keri kojiki goya

a trendy kite soars
and below . . .
a beggar's hut

乞食子や歩ながらの凧 (1820; *IZ* 1.46)
kojiki ko ya aruki nagara no ikanobori

a beggar child
walking and flying
a kite

The first example presents a hovel: a beggar's hut that we can imagine to be makeshift and pocked with holes—and yet, soaring about it is a kite: in fact, a kite of the "latest style" (*ima yō* 今様). In a later version, written in 1820, Issa changes the kite to be a "pretty" one (*utsukushiki* 美しき; *IZ* 1.46). The juxtaposition of trendy or pretty kite and a beggar's hut is powerful and highly suggestive of a non-monetary way of being rich. In the second example, a beggar child (a boy) walks along, flying a kite and, we imagine, forgetting all about his poverty and want in the splendid present moment in which a colorful kite at the end of his string twirls and dances in the sky. We might also imagine his heart soaring too—and, of course, the heart of Issa, memorializing the scene in verse.

Issa wrote scores of haiku about poor people, himself included, enjoying the riches of nature. The following poems juxtapose beggars with lotuses.

蓮の花乞食のけぶりかかる也 (1806; *IZ* 1.398)
hasu no hana kojiki no keburi kakaru nari

lotus blossoms—
the beggar's smoke
wafts over

乞食の枕に並ぶうき葉哉 (1813; *IZ* 1.398)
kojiki no makura ni narabu uki ha kana

alongside
the beggar's pillow . . .
lotus leaves float

In these scenes the beggar lives so close to the lotuses, his cooking smoke wafts over them, and the pillow where he lays his head at night nearly touches them. He may be impoverished but, Issa demonstrates without explaining, he is fortunate in his closeness to nature's splendor. The rich traditional symbolism of the lotus, producing gloriously pure flowers while floating on muddy water, contributes to a possible deeper meaning that readers can derive from these poems. Lotuses signify Buddhist enlightenment because they achieve perfection despite their rootedness in the imperfections of this world. As such, their nearness to the abodes of the beggars in these haiku hints that the latter might live close to Buddha's Pure Land—so close, they can literally reach out their hands and touch it. In this view, these beggars are fortunate indeed.

In the following example a cuckoo warbles his summer mating call, and everyone hears and enjoys—including a beggar crouched under a bridge.

時鳥橋の乞食も聞れけり (1811; *IZ* 1.339)
hototogisu hashi no kojiki mo kikare keri

a cuckoo—
the bridge beggar
listens too

Though he lives in squalor and, as Issa pointed out in an earlier haiku, is less well-off than even the most common of birds due to his lack of a proper home, the beggar listens appreciatively to the cuckoo's song. Because he lives outdoors, close to nature, and because he has no appointments or job to hurry off to, the beggar might in fact be better positioned than others, including even haiku poets, to experience on a regular, intimate basis the heart-lifting loveliness of birdsong . . . or so Issa's haiku might be understood to imply.

A beggar at a crossroads in the next example, written three months later that same year, is even more exposed to the elements, without even a bridge to shield him from the pouring summer rain.

夕立や辻の乞食が鉢の松 (1811; *IZ* 1.264)
yūdachi ya tsuji no kojiki ga hachi no matsu

rainstorm—
a crossroads beggar
with a potted pine

Nevertheless, he, too, appears not pitiful but blessed by nature in the form of a small, potted pine tree. In fact, if we interpret rainfall as a life-giving symbol, the beggar appears twice blessed: bathed by regenerative water from the heavens above while, below, nurturing a green embodiment of long life and hope. In a similar haiku, this one written over a decade later, Issa literally describes rain, in this case spring rain, as *tomi* 富: "riches, wealth, fortune."

乞食小屋富のおちけり春の雨 (1824; *IZ* 1.74)
kojiki goya tomi no ochi keri haru no ame

on a beggar's hut
riches fall . . .
spring rain

The beggar may live in a hovel, but that hovel is being washed by regenerative rain. Every drop that leaks through its holes is, in Issa's happy vision, a gem.

Beggars in Issa's haiku not only enjoy nature's free bounty; they partake fully in the national, season-based rituals of Japanese society. Instead of viewing the homeless poor (or the poor who live in hovels) as outsiders, Issa adopts a rhetoric of inclusion. Examples of this tactic are plentiful.

New Year's Day:

乞食も護摩酢酌むらん今日の春 (1795; *IZ* 1.27)
konjiki mo gomazu kumuran kyō no haru[47]

even beggars toast
with sesame sake . . .
first of spring

First Month:

乞食も福大黒のつもり哉 (1813; *IZ* 1.48)
konjiki mo fuku daikoku no tsumori kana

even the beggar
hopes to get rich . . .
god of wealth singers

Spring:

乞食も一曲あるか花の陰 (1808; *IZ* 1.210)
konjiki mo ikkyoku aru ka hana no kage

is even the beggar
singing a song?
blossom shade

Summer:

君が代は乞食の家ものぼり哉 (?[48]; *IZ* 1.288)
kimi ga yo wa kojiki no ie mo nobori kana

Great Japan!
even a beggar's house
has a summer banner

Autumn:

乞食の角力にさへも贔屓かな (1821; *IZ* 1.507)
konjiki no sumō ni sae mo hiiki kana

even for the beggar—
a favorite
wrestler

Winter:

寒声や乞食小屋の娘の子 (1822; *IZ* 1.663)
kangoe ya konjiki goya no musume no ko

winter voice drills
in the beggar's little hut . . .
little girl

In the above translations the word "even" appears in the first five examples, an English equivalent for the Japanese particle, *mo*. Issa thereby emphasizes the idea that beggars are "like the rest of us." They, too, toast the new year, hope to get rich by donating to God of Wealth Singers, sing blossom-viewing songs, display summer banners, and cheer for their favorite sumo wrestlers in autumn. And, although the sixth poem doesn't literally include an "also," this idea is very much implied—Issa's point being that a beggar girl practices winter voice drills just like other children.

In the fourth poem, interestingly, Issa opens with a phrase that by now should be familiar to readers of this study: *kimi ga yo* 君が代, an expression of praise for the emperor's reign and, by metaphorical extension, for all of "Great Japan." In other haiku, as we have seen, Issa uses this patriotic phrase to laud both the labor of peasants and service of priests, suggesting that these social groups play important roles in the material and spiritual prosperity of the nation. Here, perhaps surprisingly, he uses the same exclamation in reference to a scene in which a summer banner flies over the hovel of a beggar, a "non-human," suggesting that the beggar not only belongs in Japan because he participates in national traditions, but perhaps because, in his humble way, he contributes to the country's greatness just as farmers and priests do.

Issa's often optimistic poetic portraits of beggars expose him to the accusation that he is romanticizing poverty by stressing the "riches" of spring rain and birdsong but turning a blind eye to a devastating reality. We have already considered a poem in which a beggar child walks along, proudly flying his New Year's kite—just like his more privileged peers—reveling in the present moment and, in that moment, perhaps forgetting his misery. Issa describes similar happy moments of "kids being kids" in many other haiku, such as the following.

子ありてや橋の乞食もよぶ蛍 (1811; *IZ* 1.357)
ko arite ya hashi no kojiki mo yobu hotaru

they have kids too—
bridge beggars
calling fireflies

They may be homeless, but the family living under the bridge enjoys a summer evening game of calling to the fireflies, delighting in a sparkling, natural light show that costs them nothing. Is Issa glossing over the plight of the poor by celebrating their access to kites and fireflies? Is he romanticizing poverty in these haiku—or is he inviting readers to consider seriously the possibility that money isn't everything, and that those who have little but who can open themselves to simple pleasures and find joy in those pleasures are *truly* lucky?

In some of his haiku about beggars, especially children, Issa's optimism seems to melt away.

乞食子がおろおろ拝む雛哉 (1810; *IZ* 1.106)
kojiki ko ga oro-oro ogamu hiina kana

the beggar child prays
with trembling voice . . .
for a doll

During the Doll Festival for girls, celebrated on the third day of Third Month, other children receive lavishly dressed dolls to play with. The beggar girl, however, can only pray for one with a trembling voice . . . and be disappointed. In a similarly non-romanticized poem about beggar life, Issa calls attention to a hard fact about their existence: that, to survive, they must beg, and this difficult work begins at a tender age.

秋風や小さい声の新乞食 (1818; *IZ* 1.470)
akikaze ya chiisai koe no shin kojiki

autumn wind—
the new beggar's
small voice

乞食子や膝の上迄けさの霜 (1820; *IZ* 1.652)
kojiki ko ya hiza no ue made kesa no shimo

beggar child—
even in his lap
morning frost

In the first poem the "small voice" (*chiisai koe* 小さい声) of a "new beggar" (*shin kojiki* 新乞食) is barely heard on a day of chilly autumn wind. The cold vastness of nature as it cycles inevitably toward winter contrasts starkly with the tiny bundle of rags and life crouched by the roadside, his (or her?) tiny voice asking for alms so easily ignored by passersby. The second poem tugs even harder at the reader's heartstrings. The beggar child has gotten up so early to beg, frost has formed on the surrounding ground and even in his (or her) lap. Or, is Issa perhaps suggesting that the child has been outside, exposed to the cold, all night? In either case, the conventional association of winter with death adds great pathos to the scene, raising the question: Will this child, *can* this child, survive in this cold and indifferent world?

Perhaps Issa's own childhood experience of being an unwanted and unloved stepchild—a sort of outcast within the family unit—prepared him at an early age to view beggars with compassion, insight, and a feeling of kinship. Whatever the psychological origin of his sympathetic attitude toward the dregs of Tokugawa society, Issa remained consistent in his poetic treatment of such people, viewing them as human beings and as citizens fully involved in Japan's seasonal rituals—lucky and happy in some moments, destitute and hopeless in others. This consistently humane approach, one might note, extended for Issa beyond the human race to include all living creatures, as the companion volume to this book, *Issa and the Meaning of Animals*, demonstrates. However, it may be surprising, given the prejudices of his time, that his heart opened just as widely for the most spurned human group of all. The Ainu (*eta*) were an ethnic minority whose members lived apart from Japanese society. In the early modern period the shogun subjugated the homeland of the Ainu, the sacred hunting and fishing grounds of Ezo, which the Japanese conquerors renamed Hokkaido. In 1799, when Issa was 37, the shogun imposed direct control over Ezo's territory and people, considered barbarians by the ethnic Japanese (Walker 6; 150; 230). Though their conquered homeland was in the north, groups of Ainu lived in segregated villages throughout Japan, performing "unclean" jobs such as disposing of dead animals and people, working with leather, and executing criminals. Despite their status as the lowest caste—in effect, "outcastes"—Issa's poetic treatment of Ainu is sympathetic and perfectly matches his treatment of beggars.

> えた町に見おとされたる幟哉 (1803; *IZ* 1.288)
> *eta machi ni miotosaretaru nobori kana*
>
> in the outcastes' village
> easily overlooked . . .
> summer banners
>
> 涼しさに夜はえた村でなかりけり (1816; *IZ* 1.255)
> *suzushisa ni yo wa eta mura de nakari keri*
>
> in the evening cool
> no village
> of outcastes
>
> 正月やえたの玄関も梅の花 (1818; *IZ* 1.25)
> *shōgatsu ya eta no genkan mo ume no hana*
>
> First Month—
> even at the outcaste's porch
> plum blossoms
>
> えっ太らが家の尻より蓮の花 (1822; *IZ* 1.399)
> *ettara ga ie no shiri yori hasu no hana*
>
> from the rear
> of the outcaste's house . . .
> lotus blossoms

The Ainu in these verbal portraits fly summer banners (though easily overlooked) and enjoy nature's blessing in the form of cool breezes, blossoming plum trees, and blooming lotuses. Issa's message remains consistent even for what was considered to be the lowest rank of human life in Tokugawa Japan: nature is for all; nature makes us one. This last point is especially stressed in the second haiku. In the pleasant coolness of a summer evening, the village of outcastes simply ceases to exist, which might be interpreted to mean that social hierarchies have vanished, or at least they no longer matter in the present, transformative moment—thanks to nature's free and undiscriminating bounty.

Issa sketches beggars and Ainu with deep sympathy, celebrating their joy in happy moments, commiserating with their suffering at other times. As a man of faith who believed fervently that Amida Buddha can enable rebirth in the Pure Land for even fleas and trees, he naturally proposed the same spiritual benefit for members of society's lowest two classes.

> えた村の御講幟やお霜月 (1820; *IZ* 1.660)
> *eta mura no okō nobori ya o-shimozuki*
>
> in the outcastes' town
> a Buddhist banner . . .
> the frosty month
>
> 先立の念仏乞食や日傘 (1825; *IZ* 1.303)
> *sakidachi no nebutsu kojiki ya higarakasa*
>
> a beggar goes first
> praising Buddha . . .
> with parasol

The "frosty month" (*o-shimozuki* お霜月), that is, the Eleventh Month, meant mid-winter in the old Japanese calendar: a cold, gray, snowbound period in the mountains of Shinano. In this lifeless season Issa notes at least one bright sign of life: a Buddhist banner hinting of new birth, an enlightenment that some believers expect to occur in a remote future Pure Land, and that others expect here and now, in this world-turned-Pure Land, thanks to their awakened consciousness. Issa, who wrote many poems about touching or sensing the Pure Land in the present world, at times seems to lean toward the second group's interpretation, though it should be noted that he also refers often to physical reincarnation and the idea of an actual next-life existence in Amida's Western Paradise.[49] Regardless of how Issa personally interpreted his faith—as a promise of actual, physical rebirth or as a metaphor for awakening here and now—the Buddhist banner in this haiku, bravely displayed in the dead of winter, embodies spiritual hope, a hope that belongs as fully to the socially defined lowest grade of human being, the Ainu, as it does to everyone else. The founder of Jōdoshinshū, Shinran, would surely approve of the powerful religious statement encoded in the haiku's simple imagery. Shinran advocated an Other-Powered Buddhism that would be available even to "criminals of the highest degree, blasphemers of the Right Dharma," and "those who are utterly devoid of any stock of merit."[50] The Ainu of Japan, Issa suggests, piously follow the Buddha's path and, despite the physical cold of Shinano's winter and the symbolic cold of their countrymen's hearts, they, too, will one day reap its rewards. In the second example, a beggar strolls under a parasol in summer-time chanting the *nembutsu* ("Praise Amida Buddha!"), which, as we have noted, celebrates Amida's ego-bypassing Other Power. The praying beggar is "first" (*sakidachi* 先立), perhaps first in the temporal sense of praying early in the morning, or perhaps first in a spatial sense at the head of a procession of pilgrims. Regardless of how the reader chooses to interpret the beggar's firstness, Issa's point in the poem seems clear: Amida's Pure Land is a common aspiration and, in his belief, a common destination for all—even for the poorest of Japan's poor.

Ultimately, for Issa, rich and poor possess the same humanity and enjoy the same possibility of achieving enlightenment. A haiku about an unlikely musical duet perhaps best sums up his Buddhist-inspired social vision.

玉琴も乞食の笛もかすみけり (1808; *IZ* 1.83)
tamagoto mo kojiki no fue mo kasumi keri

a precious harp
a beggar's flute
deep in mist

The courtier and a beggar play different instruments, but music is music, and the spring mist that covers them, covers them equally.

In addition to beggars, outcastes, and (as mentioned in the previous chapter) prostitutes, another group of people existing outside of the officially recognized ranks of society—that is to say, another group derisively labeled *hinin* or nonhuman—was the criminal class. While Issa doesn't devote a lot of attention to this class in his poetry, from time to time he makes references to them, in particular to thieves. In a few cases, he alludes to famous robbers of Japanese history, such as Kumasaka, whose name translates to "Bear Hill": a robber chief of the closing years of the Heian period (794-1185). Issa wrote three fanciful haiku about Kumasaka's halberd in connection with fireflies (1811; *IZ* 1.357), with autumn wind (1813; *IZ* 1.469), and with hailstones (1813; *IZ* 1.648). Benten-kozuo, a legendary robber depicted in an Edo-period kabuki play, *Shiranami gonin otoko* ("White Waves, Five Men"), also finds his way into a haiku by Issa, in which he plays "the dandy with a pipe" under cherry blossoms (1818; *IZ* 1.215). Such poems, however, are more like humorous literary exercises than portraits of human life, for they reveal nothing about contemporary criminals. However, in a handful of other poems Issa focuses on some actual early modern thieves. In 1810, on the sixth day of Fourth Month, he witnessed the capture and punishment of one such thief, and he wrote the following haiku about the experience.

> 行々し下手盗人をはやすらん (1810; *IZ* 1.351)
> *gyōgyōshi heta nusubito wo hayasuran*
>
> cheered on
> by a reed thrush
> the incompetent thief

In a prose note for this poem Issa explains that a man attempted to steal a robe but was caught by the local citizens of Takawa, tied to a bamboo pole, and run out of town—a spectacle that the poet goes on to describe as "entertaining" (*kyō* 興; *IZ* 2.572). In the poem a warbling reed thrush seems to join in the noise and excitement of the townspeople. In this particular depiction of a "man who steals" (*nusubito* 盗人), albeit an incompetent one, Issa indicates no degree of sympathy for the culprit, as he celebrates the village's swift justice of which even a bird approves.

In a pair of haiku with a more serious tone, Issa juxtaposes a thief with moonlight.

> 泥坊や其身そのまま朧月 (1816; *IZ* 1.81)
> *dorobō ya sono mi sono mama oboro-zuki*
>
> the thief
> is just as he is . . .
> hazy moon

> 御十夜は巾着切も月夜也 (1819; *IZ* 1.657)
> *o-jūya wa kinchakukiri mo tsuki yo nari*

> winter prayers—
> a cutpurse, too
> in moonlight

In the first haiku the season word, *oboro* 朧, refers to spring haze. The night robber, Issa notes, is "just as he is" (*sono mi sono mama* 其身そのまま). Evidently because of the haze, the thief feels no need to hide in some dark corner; he can simply act naturally, just how he is. Or, perhaps Issa's implication is that the thief's presence on a foggy night is perfectly natural, an inevitable part of the scene. If we interpret the poem in this way, the thief belongs here, just as much as the haze and the moonlight do. The second example, written three years later, can be read in a similar fashion. On a night of winter prayers, part of a ten-night, Tenth Month religious observance during which Pure Land Buddhists chant the *nembutsu*, a cut-purse or, in more modern terms, a pickpocket is also present, as much a part of the moonlit scene as the devout Buddhists whom he is robbing. As noted earlier, the founder of Issa's sect of Buddhism, Shinran, insisted that even criminals might be reborn in the Pure Land, thanks to Amida Buddha's Original Vow. Since this is the case, the cutpurse mingling with the chanting throng is just as able as the most devout among them to one day realize the benefits of their prayer.

The previous haiku appeared in Issa's journal *Hachiban nikki* in Sixth Month of 1819. Later that same year, in Twelfth Month, he wrote the following haiku in the same notebook.

> 雪降や夜盗も鼻を明の方 (1819; *IZ* 1.34)
> *yuki furu ya yatō mo hana wo ake no hō*

> with snow falling
> the night thief must follow his nose too . . .
> New Year's walk

This haiku refers to the New Year's custom of visiting a shrine or temple located in a lucky direction. However, in a thickly falling snow it's difficult for a pilgrim to see the landmarks that would aid him or her in staying on course. Each person now must, literally, follow his or her nose—and hope for the best. In his poem Issa imagines how the scene might appear from the perspective of a night thief. All of us, Issa suggests, are subject to nature, and, because we are part of nature, we can perceive only as well as natural conditions permit. Everyone must follow his or her nose; everyone will go astray now and then. The thief, in this poetic scene, is simply being one of us, simply being human.

In another poem, Issa addresses a *ryōjō no kunshi* 梁上の君子: an archaic word for a burglar.

梁上の君子も見やれ草の露 (1821; *IZ* 1.483)
ryōjō no kunshi mo mi yare kusa no tsuyu

you look too
robber! dewdrops
in the grass

The person may be a thief, but Issa implies that he is a human being as well: open to enjoying the sparkling wonder of a morning field shimmering with dew. The time of day is significant. Presumably, the robber has been busy all night, plying his trade, but now, at sunrise, the glorious scene of dewdrops shines for him, "too" (*mo*). The feeling in the poem is positive and inclusive. Beyond this, the fact that dewdrops are a conventional Buddhist symbol for impermanence—the notion that nothing in this world abides—might imply that Issa is gently reminding the robber to confront reality and understand that any riches stolen the night before are no more permanent than the dew that the mid-morning sun will burn and evaporate, no more permanent than anyone's life. Once again, Issa voices a sentiment that perfectly aligns with Shinran's teaching: even a criminal can be awakened spiritually, if only he opens his eyes to the real.

In other haiku about thieves, Issa waxes less philosophical.

盗人のかすんでげけら笑ひかな　(1822; *IZ* 1.88)
nusubito no kasunde gekera warai kana

in thick spring mist
the burglar
laughing

大とびや逃盗人と時鳥　(1825; *IZ* 1.346)
ōtobi ya nige nusubito to hototogisu

a big leap—
the fleeing burglar
and a cuckoo

とびくらをするや夜盗と時鳥　(1825; *IZ* 1.346)
tobikura wo suru ya yatō to hototogisu

having a flying contest
a night burglar
a cuckoo

In the first example, a burglar laughs in the thick mist, rejoicing in the cover for his crimes that nature has provided. The poem can be read in many ways. Perhaps Issa is merely remarking, sarcastically, that the mist is so thick that only a burglar would appreciate it. Or else, perhaps he is simply seeing reality from the thief's point of view—which shouldn't surprise readers familiar with Issa's many haiku in which he strives to imagine the perspectives of fleas, flies, and frogs. The burglar in the second and third examples, written in the same year, leaps or "flies" off a roof at the same moment that a cuckoo takes off. Issa humorously compliments the thief's ability to soar.

Although he wrote only a handful of haiku about criminals, Issa envisions them in much the same way as he envisions people of other walks of life. Some are incompetent (and suffer for it), and others are successful—hidden by the same thick mist that enwraps the most upright of citizens. He playfully praises the flying ability of one but urges another to notice and pay attention to the dewdrops of dawn and to the Buddhist lesson that they embody. Even a cutpurse preying on a temple crowd on a night of winter prayers might enjoy the benefit of the saving Other Power that those prayers celebrate, Issa implies. Once again, as he does consistently in his haiku that explore what it means to be human, Issa suggests that, down deep, despite social differences or even seemingly important factors such as one's poverty, homelessness, or socially imposed status as an outcaste; there is no such thing as a "non-human" person, no such thing as a demonized "other."

Chapter 9. THE OLD

In early modern Japan Confucian values imported from China, including a quasi-religious reverence for elderly family members, remained important.

古ばばが丸める餅の口伝哉 (1822; *IZ* 1.675)
furu baba ga marumeru mochi no kuden kana

old granny teaches
her secret . . .
rice cakes perfectly round

The old woman in this haiku teaches a kitchen trick to, presumably, a younger female relative. "Old granny" (*furu baba* 古ばば) appears as a respect-worthy font of knowledge in the poem, generously passing that knowledge on to the next generation. Confucius would approve. However, if Confucius were to thumb through Issa's pages seeking similar poems presenting old people as saintly figures worthy of adulation, he would be sorely disappointed. Confucian reverence fails to emerge as a significant theme in Issa's poems about the elderly.

Issa rarely idealizes old people in his haiku portraits of them. Instead, he documents and reflects on their physical and mental conditions based on direct observation and his own personal experience of the aging process, writing poems about their acute sensitivity to cold weather, about their lowered sex drive, about their loss of teeth, their wrinkles, and their loss of memory. He also explores certain unchanging aspects of the old, for example the abiding and deepened appreciation for nature's beauty that many of them manifest. He presents happy images of old people enjoying spring blossoms, and pathetic images of old people who still must work hard to survive, despite their growing infirmities. Finally, as we shall learn in this chapter, Priest Issa reflects on the meaning of old age in terms of his Buddhist understanding of death and what death means.

An early reference to a physiological change related to aging occurs in a haiku of 1792, when Issa was only thirty.

翁さびうしろをあぶるほた火哉 (1792; *IZ* 1.707)
okinasabi ushiro wo aburu hotabi kana

an old man's ways—
my backside warmed
by the wood fire

The man has tucked up his kimono, exposing his backside to a cozy-warm fire, an action described as *okinasabi* 翁さび: typical of the elderly.[51] Although a first-person pronoun doesn't appear in the Japanese text, the poem becomes more humorous (hence more Issa-like and more Issa-worthy) if we imagine that the person behaving like an oldster is the thirty year-old poet. This interpretation has guided my English translation. If the haiku is indeed a comic self-portrait, Issa may be making fun of the fact that already at age thirty he's behaving like an old man and describing himself in those terms.

In many other haiku, such as the next two examples, Issa depicts old people who, due to their slower metabolism, naturally abhor cold weather.

初雪に聞おじしたる翁哉 (1803; *IZ* 1.634)
hatsu yuki ni kiku ojishitaru okina kana

hearing of first snow
a dreadful thing . . .
old man

爺が世や枯木も雪の花の春 (1825; *IZ* 1.28)
jiji ga yo ya kare-gi mo yuki no hana no haru

an old man's world—
flowers of snow on bare trees
spring's blossoms

Many haiku poets look forward eagerly to the year's first snowfall, an occasion for composing verses, but not the "old man" in the poem of 1803, possibly a sketch of Issa himself at age forty-one. The coldness of the winter season that the first snowfall announces is "a dreadful thing" for the old man in question not only because of physical discomfort but also due to the fact that winter is a physically taxing endur-ance test that many old people will not pass. In the later haiku of 1825, written when Issa was sixty-three, tree branches are bare, and snow is falling or has fallen, but an old man dreams of springtime. Issa alludes here to a Japanese folktale, "Hanasaka Jiijii" (花咲か爺)—also called "Hanasaka Jiisan" (花咲か爺さん)—in which an old man makes cherry trees magically bloom by sprinkling ashes on them, following the advice of the ghost of his faithful family dog (that was treacherously killed by a neighbor). The evil neighbor is eventually punished in the tale, and the old man is blessed with the magical ability to hurry up the blooming of a cherry tree—by implication, to hurry up the coming of spring. In the story's happy ending, a daimyo passes by, impressed by the old man's miracle, and showers him with gifts. Issa's point in alluding to this tale is that winter is no season for the old. If only he had the power of the old man in the story and could exchange blossoms for snow, spring for winter, he would do so. The tone of the haiku is light, but the symbolic linkage of winter with death (bare branches as opposed to blooming branches) is ominous. Every winter an old person must wonder if he or she will live to see, once again, spring's blossoms and to feel, once again, the warmth of the spring sun.

In another haiku Issa makes the poetic connection between the coming of cold weather and the coming of death even more overt.

秋風や翌捨らるる姥が顔 (1817; *IZ* 1.470)
akikaze ya asu suteraruru uba ga kao

autumn wind—
tomorrow they throw you away
old woman

The poem refers to Mount Sarashina, also known as Mount Ubasute or Obasute: a mountain in Shinano Province where, according to legend (perhaps with some historical truth to it), old people once were "thrown away" (*ubasute* 姥捨): left to die in times when food was scarce. In the last phrase Issa focuses on an "old woman's face" (*uba ga kao* 姥が顔), which we can imagine to be not only wrinkled but also reddened by the chilly autumn wind. Tomorrow, he predicts, the woman will be thrown away, just as old people in ancient times were discarded on Mount Sarashina so as not deprive the young of food. Such abandonment, according to folklore, was an act of supreme sacrifice: the old heroically dying so that the young might live. Issa's haiku however, contains no hint of this noble purpose. Instead, the coldness of the wind matches the coldness of a reality in which a solitary old woman will very soon die and not be missed. As far as society is concerned, she will be "thrown away" like so much rubbish.[52]

Given the physical hardship caused by colder months, old people in Issa's haiku naturally rejoice at the arrival of warmer seasons.

としよりの今を春辺や夜の雨 (1808; *IZ* 1.58)
toshiyori no ima wo harube ya yoru no ame

now it's a springtime
befitting old men . . .
evening rain

蚊もちらりほらり是から老が世ぞ (1819; *IZ* 1.370)
ka mo chirari horari kore kara oi ga yo zo

a smattering of mosquitoes—
from today on
an old man's world

The arrival of spring, celebrated in the first poem, and the arrival of summer, signaled by mosquitoes in the second, inspire a special joy for the elderly. In contrast to the ominous tone in Issa's poems about the aged in autumn and winter, these spring and summer haiku are light and celebratory. Old folks have survived another winter and can therefore rejoice and enjoy "their" time.

In addition to loathing cold weather for its discomfort and dreading it for its association with death—both real and symbolic—old people in Issa's haiku portraits demonstrate other attitudes and dispositions popularly associated with the physical changes of aging, one of these being a lowered sex drive. In the following poems, the "old man" in question is their author at ages fifty-seven and sixty-three, respectively.

とし寄りの袖としらでや虎が雨 (1819; *IZ* 1.262)
toshiyori no sode to shirade ya tora ga ame

unknowingly wetting
an old man's sleeves . . .
Rain of the Tiger

としよりのおれが袖へも虎が雨 (1825; *IZ* 1.263)
toshiyori no ore ga sode e mo tora ga ame

wetting this old man's
sleeve too . . .
Rain of the Tiger

According to tradition, if it rains on the 28th day of Fifth Month, the raindrops, magically, are the tears shed by Lady Tora ("Tiger"), the concubine or, according to some sources, the wife of one of the Soga brothers who famously avenged their father's murder on that day in 1193. The brothers, Jurō and Gorō, killed Kudō Suketsune during a hunting party on Mount Fuji. Jurō died in the battle; Gorō was later executed for the deed. Nobuyuki Yuasa notes, "When the elder brother [Gorō] parted from his wife Tora before setting out with his brother to kill Suketsune, her tears were so copious that ever after rain fell on that day" (Kobayashi Issa, *The Year of My Life* 75). In both of these haiku, Issa humorously observes that the young woman's tears for her lover are falling on the wrong person: on himself, an old man. He comically implies that his time for passionate love has long passed and yet, ironically and incongruously, he finds himself caught in its rain. A possible deeper implication, however, is that despite his age the old man in the scene still cannot escape the influence of erotic passion embodied in the raindrop-tears. The flesh may be weak, but the spirit may still be willing.

Issa also poetically reflects upon, and comically mines, the topic of tooth loss.

初霜や茎の歯ぎれも去年迄 (1806; *IZ* 1.650)
hatsu shimo ya kuki no hagire mo kyonen made

first frost—
my teeth could crack radishes
up to last year

In this, one of his many haiku in which he laments his loss of teeth, Issa remembers with poignant regret that up to the previous year he could crack tough "stem vegetables" (*kuki* 茎) with his teeth . . . but no longer. Although the poem's seasonal reference, "first frost," might be read metaphorically as "first step toward death"—given the archetypal association between winter and dying—Issa discovers comedy in the situation, presenting himself as the butt of a cosmic joke being played by life itself. Six years later, he continues in the same vein.

花げしのふはつくやふな前歯哉 (1812; *IZ* 1.392)
hana-geshi no fuwatsuku yōna maeba kana

like a poppy
how it sways . . .
front tooth

When he composed this haiku in 1812, Issa was fifty. Japanese critic, Yoshida Miwako, believes that the swaying tooth in question (*fuwatsuku* ふはつく: unstable, wavering) must be the poet's, an interpretation that makes the verse a rather light-hearted, autobiographical reflection on the aging process (188). If so, this haiku of 1812 is a memory piece, since—according to Issa's poetic diary, *Shichiban nikki*—on the 16th day of Sixth Month of the previous year (1811), "Issa's one tooth fell out" (*IZ* 3.121). Toothless by age forty-nine, the poet had good cause to consider himself an "old man" at a point that seems middle age by today's standards.

Issa confronts tooth loss and aging with self-ironic humor in many other haiku, including the following.

> 葉固の歯一枚もなかりけり (1819; *IZ* 1.49)
> *hagatame no ha ichi mai mo nakari keri*
>
> New Year's tooth-hardening
> meal . . .
> yet toothless!

> 台所の爺に歯固勝れけり (1821; *IZ* 1.49)
> *daidoko no jiji ni hagatame katare keri*
>
> old man in the kitchen—
> his New Year's tooth-hardening
> beats mine

> 歯固は猫に勝れて笑ひけり (?; *IZ* 1.49)
> *hagatame wa neko ni katarete warai keri*
>
> New Year's tooth-hardening
> meal . . . the cat wins
> and laughs

All three poems refer to a special tooth-hardening dish traditionally eaten during the New Year's season. In the first, Issa reflects on the absurdity of a toothless man eating the supposedly tooth-protecting rice cake. In the second haiku the sorry state of Issa's teeth (in other words, his complete lack of them) is magnified by the fact that some other "old man" (*jiji* 爺) has a more complete set. In the third example, a cat, possessing good, hard teeth, seems to be laughing at the dentally challenged poet.

Another physical change associated with aging, the wrinkling of once smooth and supple skin, also finds its way into Issa's poetic observations.

同じ年の顔の皺見ゆる灯籠哉 (1803; *IZ* 1.493)
onaji toshi no kao no shiwa miyuru tōro kana

a wrinkled face
he's my age . . .
lanterns for the dead

Issa was forty-one when he wrote this haiku, once again suggesting that he identified as an old man, at least in his poetic self-portraits, at a relatively early age. The Bon Festival of the Dead takes place in Eighth Month in the old Japanese calendar. At this time, people light lanterns to guide their ancestors' spirits back home. In this highly evocative verse, two faces are illuminated by the lanterns for the dead: Issa's and another person's. The other person is Issa's age, but his face, in the lantern light, looks deeply wrinkled. The haiku captures a startling discovery that might be paraphrased, "This other guy who looks so wrinkled and old in the flickering light is *my* age!" The seasonal setting, the Festival for the Dead, underscores the fact that the two wrinkled people in the scene, Issa and his companion, are moving inexorably toward a time in the not-so distant future when these lanterns will be lit for them.

The sight of wrinkles and thoughts of death are linked in other haiku as well.

手の皺の一夜に見ゆる秋の雨 (1804; *IZ* 1.465)
te no shiwa no hito yo ni miyuru aki no ame

all night looking
at my wrinkled hands . . .
autumn rain

見上皺見下ル皺の夜寒哉 (1816; *IZ* 1.436)
mi-age shiwa mi-sagaru shiwa no yozamu kana

    looking up, wrinkles
    looking down, wrinkles . . .
    a cold night

On a chilly night of autumn rain, Issa looks at his wrinkled hands—and says nothing more about the experience, allowing his readers to connect the seasonal context with aging and thoughts of mortality. The second example, also highly suggestive, again relies on readers to finish it. Issa simply provides the image of contemplating wrinkles (his own, one might presume) on a cold winter's night. Readers are free to take this evocative, unexplained image and meditate on what it might mean to the poet and to themselves personally on their own paths to old age and life's inevitable ending.

    In other haiku about wrinkles, Issa strikes a lighter tone.

    ほた焚て皺くらべせんかがみ山 (1805; *IZ* 1.708)
    hota taite shiwa kurabesen kagami yama

    by the wood fire
    comparing our wrinkles . . .
    Mount Kagami

    梅干と皺くらべせんはつ時雨 (1806; *IZ* 1.621)
    umeboshi to shiwa kurabesen hatsu shigure

    comparing my wrinkles
    with the pickled plums . . .
    first winter rain

In the first example the setting is Mount Kagami in Saga Prefecture near the resort city of Karatsu, and the time is winter—indicated by the seasonal reference to a wood fire. In this cold world on a cold mountain, two old men huddle by a fire, comparing (Issa humorously notes) their wrinkles.

While the coldness of the season intimates the coldness of approaching death, the attitude in the haiku is quite playful: perhaps each man believes that the other looks more wrinkled than he; or, perhaps, they realize that there can and will be no winner in this contest. In the second poem "pickled plum" (*umeboshi* 梅干) is an idiom that can denote an old, wrinkled woman. However, in a later haiku Issa uses it to describe old men.

> 梅見るや梅干爺と呼れつつ (1822; *IZ* 1.204)
> *ume miru ya umeboshi jijii to yobaretsutsu*
>
> viewing plum blossoms—
> they call old men
> pickled plums

In the haiku of 1806 the imminence of death is suggested by the winter rain, but the comparison of the poet's wrinkles to a shriveled-up plum is amusing and self-ironic. The 1822 poem makes the same comic link between old men and *umeboshi* in a springtime context of viewing plum blossoms. The plum blossoms, symbolizing youth, and the dried-up plum-faced men, symbolizing age, coexist in a scene that I choose to imagine to be a happy one.

Wrinkles also figure in haiku about tiny insects to which they might appear, Issa imagines, to be deep furrows.

> 手の皺が歩み悪いか初蛍 (1807; *IZ* 1.356)
> *te no shiwa ga arumi nikui ka hatsu-botaru*
>
> is my wrinkled hand
> bad for walking?
> first firefly
>
> 手の皺に蹴つまづいたる蛍かな (1815; *IZ* 1.359)
> *te no shiwa ni ketsu mazuitaru hotaru kana*

tripping
on the wrinkles of my hand . . .
firefly

In these intimate close-ups Issa tries to imagine what he and his wrinkles must look like to the firefly. The feeling in these poems is one of tender concern; with mock-seriousness Issa apologizes for the inconvenience that his wrinkled hands are posing for the firefly that has alit on them. Issa's age and his sense of his own mortality add to the tenderness of the moment.

皺腕歩きあきてや蚤のとぶ (1813; *IZ* 1.377)
shiwa kaina aruki akite ya nomi no tobu

tired of walking
on my wrinkled arm
the flea jumps

群蠅の逃げた跡打皺手哉 (1821; *IZ* 1.375)
mure-bae no nigeta ato utsu shiwade kana

after the fly swarm
escapes, swat!
my wrinkled hand

The last example contains two references to aging: the poet's wrinkles and his slow reflexes, swatting at a fly after it has already flown away. In all of these examples Issa's tone is comic and self-ironic; he seems cheerfully resigned to the inescapable fact that he has grown old.

Whereas he at times finds comedy in old people's aversion to the cold, in their waning sex drive, in their loss of teeth, and in their gaining of wrinkles; Issa portrays an additional change associated with aging with great pathos.

年寄の腰や花見の迷子札 (1821; *IZ* 1.217)
toshiyori no koshi ya hanami no maigo fuda

around the old man's waist
blossom viewing . . .
a name tag

花さくや爺が腰の迷子札 (?; *IZ* 1.217)
hana saku ya jiji ga koshi no maigo fuda

cherry blossoms—
around grandpa's waist
a name tag

Maigo fuda has two meanings: one is a sign announcing a lost child, the other a name tag on a person to prevent him or her from getting lost. The latter meaning applies in these haiku. The old man evidently suffers from memory loss serious enough to require him to wear a name tag. The fact that he evidently suffers from Alzheimer's casts a shadow over what would normally be a bright, happy scene of people enjoying the blossoming cherry trees. However, the overall effect perhaps isn't completely dark. The poem involves provocative tensions—sadness and delight, old age and springtime, decay and regeneration—thereby raising questions that every reader must answer for him or herself. Does the old man's deteriorating mental condition make the poem, in total, depressing, or does his presence among his fellow blossom-viewers, despite his disability, make the haiku more of a celebration of an undying love for nature—even in the heart of an old man who can't remember his own name? Should the reader focus on the possibility that the man is enjoying, perhaps for the last time, the sweet, comforting, and familiar beauty of the blossoms; or focus on the man's debilitating and irreversible loss of mental faculties? Issa leaves these questions for his reader to ponder.

In less emotionally ambiguous haiku, Issa notes that a deep love for, and excitement over, spring blossoms continues even for the old.

山桜花きちがひの爺哉 (1812; *IZ* 1.228)
yama-zakura hana kichigai no jijii kana

he's a mountain
cherry blossom-crazed
old man

桜へと見えてじんじんばしより哉 (1818; *IZ* 1.231)
sakura e to miete jin-jin bashiyori kana

off to view cherry blossoms
old man with kimono
tucked

としよりも目の正月ぞさくら花 (?; *IZ* 1.234)
toshiyori mo me no shōgatsu zo sakura hana

even an old man
has New Year's eyes . . .
cherry blossoms

The old men in these poems continue to delight in spring's blossoms, despite their mounting years. The second example requires a bit of explanation. The phrase *jin-jin bashiyori* じんじんばしより refers to lifting the back hem of a kimono and tucking it into the obi sash at the waist, allowing for more freedom of movement. The result is a bouncing, dynamic, and happy image. The blossoms function as a sort of Fountain of Youth for the old man, infusing him with so much energy that he tucks up his kimono so that he can rush to see them. Their beauty has turned back the clock, returning the man to the state of the child: restoring his childlike awe at the natural beauty on Planet Earth. In the third example, the sight of cherry blossoms puts an old man (Issa?) in a gleeful, "First Month" mood—reminding us once again that in the Tokugawa Japanese calendar New Year's Day was also the first day of spring. This is an undated revision of a haiku written in 1823. The original poem started with *kochitora mo* こちとらも ("we"; *IZ* 1.234). Issa decided to substitute "old man" for "we," creating, once again, the poetically evocative juxtaposition of old man and fresh, new blossoms found in other works.

In the next two examples the poet again describes the season of blossoms as an "old man's world" (*oi ga yo* 老が世).

老が世に桃太郎も出よ桃の花 (1816; *IZ* 1.236)
oi ga yo ni momotarō mo deyo momo no hana

in a world for the old
Peach Boy too, emerge!
peach blossoms

老が世に桃太郎も出よ捨瓢 (1816; *IZ* 1.593)
oi ga yo ni momotarō mo deyo sute fukube

in a world for the old
Peach Boy too, emerge!
hollow gourd

These haiku were composed in Second Month and Eighth Month of 1816, respectively. In keeping with their times of composition, the first has a spring seasonal reference ("peach blossoms") while the second evokes autumn ("gourd"). Both poems allude to the folktale of the Peach Boy. According to the story, a childless woman was washing clothes in a stream one day when she spotted a huge peach floating by in the current. She grabbed it and brought it home. When she and her husband cut open the giant fruit, they found a little boy inside: Momotarō, "Peach Boy" (see Blyth 2.418). In the first poem, Issa playfully invites Peach Boy to come outside to enjoy (appropriately) the peach blossoms. The command, "emerge!" (*deyo* 出よ), could mean to go outside of one's house or, more probably in the context of the folktale, to emerge from the giant peach—in other words, to be miraculously born (again) in this "world for the old," that is, springtime. In the second poem, Issa ends his exhortation to Peach Boy with the image of a hollow gourd, suggesting that the boy has heeded the poet's call and has come out of his shell, a gourd substituting for the peach of the myth. However, because it is now autumn, the spring revelry of old people is long over. The empty gourd serves as a melancholy reminder of past warmth, past youth.

In addition to still enjoying spring blossoms, old folks in Issa's haiku portraits also still manifest a competitive spirit, which prompts them, at times, to rejoice in victory.

> 勝声や花咲爺が菊の花 (1814; *IZ* 1.557)
> *kachi-goe ya hana saku jiji ga kiku no hana*
>
> a victory shout—
> the old man's chrysanthemum
> has won!
>
> 勝菊にほろりと爺が涙哉 (1814; *IZ* 1.557)
> *kachi kiku ni horori to jiji ga namida kana*
>
> a prize-winning chrysanthemum!
> the old man
> weeps

The jubilant old man in these haiku, both written in Ninth Month of 1814, is plainly Issa at age fifty-two. In *Shichiban nikki* the first poem has the headnote, "Potted Chrysanthemum-Growing Contest" (*kiku awase* 菊合; *IZ* 3.333). His exultation upon winning first prize with his flower suggests that despite his wrinkles and missing teeth, the heart within him hasn't changed; his victory cry erupts and his tears of joy flow as spontaneously as they did in bygone days.

Some of Issa's haiku images of old people have a satirical bite.

> としよりの追従わらひや花の陰 (1803; *IZ* 1.208)
> *toshiyori no tsuisho warai ya hana no kage*
>
> an old man's
> flattering laughter . . .
> blossom shade
>
> 翌の夜の月を請合ふ爺かな (1821; *IZ* 1.453)
> *asu no yo no tsuki wo ukeau jijii kana*
>
> "tomorrow night
> the harvest moon!"
> old man's promise

The setting of the first poem is a cherry blossom-viewing party. A group has gathered in the "blossom shade" (*hana no kage* 花の陰) to enjoy natural beauty, camaraderie, and, most probably, libations of sake. Issa focuses on one old man among the company, whose laughter stands out as being noticeably "flattering" (*tsuisho* 追従) . . . a bit *too* flattering, perhaps. Instead of displaying taciturn dignity, the old man in question tries to blend in with his younger colleagues. The haiku pokes fun at the old man (who, as always, could be the poet), clearly not acting his age. In an era in which an "affected laugh" was considered, at least by one samurai source, to indicate "lack of self-respect in a man and lewdness in a woman," the old man in the scene appears especially pitiful and ridiculous (Yamamoto 32). The old person in the second poem is annoying in a different way: needlessly predicting the next day's harvest moon, a fact that everyone must already know. Or, perhaps he's predicting clear weather that will allow the moon to be seen on the following night. In either case, Issa gently satirizes the propensity of know-it-all old people to spout their knowledge or, worse, their baseless opinions—whether those around them want to hear them or not.

A haiku about an old woman might also be a satirical jab.

夕顔の花で洟かむおばば哉 [53] (1819; *IZ* 1.391)
yūgao no hana de hana kamu o-baba kana

blowing her snot
on the moonflower . . .
granny

This poem, appearing in *Oraga haru* in 1819, is a rewrite of an almost identical haiku, written in *Shichiban nikki* in 1812. In the original version, the nose-blowing culprit was a "young girl" (*musume* 娘), suggesting that this kind of unbecoming behavior has no age limit. The image of an old woman behaving indifferently to nature's beauty seems more damning than that of a young girl doing the same; the old woman should know better. Her use of the delicate flower as tissue paper might lead some readers to interpret the revised poem to be a critique of old people's self-centeredness. However, one might alternatively choose to view granny's action as evidence that the elderly have lived long enough to no longer care about social decorum. After a lifetime of following the rules of etiquette and fulfilling her gender role by always acting demure and self-effacing, the old woman now, at last, blows her nose without caring in the least what others (including Issa or his readers) might think of her. Her desecration of the moonflower thus becomes her declaration of independence. Other poems seem to reinforce this interpretation.

さく花にぶつきり棒の翁哉 (1810; *IZ* 1.211)
saku hana ni bukkiribō no okina kana

amid cherry blossoms
he speaks bluntly . . .
old man

婆々どのが酒呑に行く月よ哉 (1811; *IZ* 1.451)
baba dono ga sake nomi ni yuku tsukiyo kana

granny walks along
drinking sake . . .
a moonlit night

In the first haiku, the old man talks "plainly" or "bluntly" (*bukkiribō* ぶつきり棒)—no flattering laughter from *him!* He says what he thinks, and he makes no attempt to sugarcoat or self-censor. In the second, granny boldly swigs her sake in public without concern for what anyone else may think of her. These old people, Issa implies, have reached a point in their lives at which they are no longer tightly bound to the strict social protocols of Tokugawa Japan. They can blow their noses on flowers, bluntly speak their minds, and guzzle sake in public to their hearts' content, because their age including all the dues that they paid over many, many years have permitted this.

Striking a less humorous and less happy note are Issa's several haiku depictions of poor people who must continue to work despite their old age. These three examples are typical:

春風やおばは四十九でしなの道 (1817; *IZ* 1.77)
haru kaze ya oba wa shijūku de shinano michi

spring breeze—
forty-nine old women
on the Shinano road

としよりもあれ出代るぞことし又 (1822; *IZ* 1.105)
toshiyori mo are degawaru zo kotoshi mata

old men
among the migrating servants . . .
this year too

婆どのの目がねをかけて茶つみ哉 (1822; *IZ* 1.114)
baba dono no megane wo kakete cha tsumi kana

granny puts on
her spectacles . . .
tea picking

In the springtime, old servants in Edo and other urban centers were replaced by young ones. The two groups would pass each other on the road: the old returning to their home villages, the young migrating to cities. In the first two examples, old women and men are perhaps returning to their homes after a lifetime of hard labor in exile—tragic enough—or perhaps, even more tragically, they are traveling in the direction of Edo or some other city in search of work. Issa allows the reader to draw his or her own conclusions, but in either interpretation these poor, elderly laborers trudging on weary legs must inspire compassion. In the third haiku, an old woman puts on her glasses to allow her to see well enough to harvest tea leaves. Her eyesight is failing, but her need to work continues.

As we noted in Chapter 1, Issa associated the primary consciousness of the very young with a kind of open, accepting mindset that seems to be a necessary requirement for Buddhist enlightenment. Interestingly, he at times also associates old people with spontaneous and sincere religious devotion and action, suggesting that the course of human life might ideally complete a full circle in which the ending and beginning are experientially similar.

> 門前の爺が作し灌仏ぞ (1816; *IZ* 1.281)
> *monzen no jiji ga tsukurishi kuwanbutsu zo*
>
> before the gate
> an old man's homemade
> birthday Buddha
>
> 婆々どのも牛に引かれて桜かな (1822; *IZ* 1.233)
> *baba dono mo ushi ni hikarete sakura kana*
>
> granny comes too
> led by a cow . . .
> cherry blossoms

In the old Japanese calendar, Buddha's birthday was celebrated on the 8th day of Fourth Month. The old man in the first poem (Issa at fifty-four?) has made his own little shrine, like the one displayed in temples, evincing a simple, trusting, childlike devotion—the kind of non-calculating faith recommended by Shinran. In the second poem, an old woman is led by a cow to a grove of blooming cherry trees, an image filled with religious significance. The haiku alludes to a popular folktale in Issa's home province of Shinano about a sinful woman who left a piece of cloth to dry in the garden behind her house, until a passing cow snagged it with a horn and trotted off. The woman followed the beast all the way to Zenkōji, where it disappeared and she found herself standing before the image of Amida Buddha. From that point on, she became pious. In two earlier haiku (1803, 1811) Issa presents images of cows leading a person to Zenkōji, but he cleverly twists this poem of 1822 to have the cow lead the old woman not to Amida's temple but to a grove of blooming cherry trees. Nature thus replaces, symbolically, the temple, which makes the woman's unplanned flower-viewing excursion a sort of holy pilgrimage. The old woman didn't set out to see the blossoms that could symbolize enlightenment; instead, she has simply followed an errant cow and now, suddenly, finds herself immersed in a terrestrial Pure Land. Like the old man who built his own shrine to baby Buddha, the old woman behaves more like a playful, spontaneous child than a serious, calculating adult. At the end of life's journey, Issa implies, some lucky individuals rediscover exactly what they knew at its very beginning: how to simply open themselves to the present moment and to the Other Power of the Buddha that has nothing to do with a remote future life but has everything to do with a profound spiritual awakening, here and now.

CONCLUSION: THE PROMISE OF POPPIES

We began this study by considering a haiku that, due to a perhaps deliberate ambiguity in Issa's word choice, can be understood in two distinct ways.

なかなかに人と生れて秋の暮 (1811; *IZ* 6.31)
naka-naka ni hito to umarete aki no kure

quite remarkable
being born human . . .
autumn dusk

just so-so
being born human . . .
autumn dusk

Human existence for Issa is remarkable; human existence for Issa is "so-so": a "middling" or "in-between" state. These two interpretations would appear to be mutually exclusive, but perhaps they are not. Perhaps being born human is remarkable precisely because it's not a lofty, special existence. People, as our survey of Issa's haiku has shown, are born into the thick of this natural universe, not above it, below it, or off to the side. In his poetic vision samurai, priests, and merchants bow together to the blossoms of spring and the moon of autumn; a daimyo respectfully dismounts his horse in the presence of cherry blossoms; a sumo champion releases a sparrow with an apology; and merchants use account books for pillows on hot or cool summer days. Being human in the sense of existing in the midst of nature *is* truly remarkable. In 1812, Issa composed a series of haiku devoted to the Six Ways of Buddhist incarnation in which the verse describing human existence is quite revealing in the context of this discussion.

さく花の中にうごめく衆生哉 (1812; *IZ* 1.212)
saku hana no naka ni ugomeku shujō kana

squirming
through the cherry blossoms . . .
people

To be human, Issa suggests, means to "squirm" (*ugomeku* うごめく) like worms through a world of fragile, temporary beauty. On one level, the haiku is a humorous jab at the annoying hoards of people who infest spring groves for cherry blossom-viewing parties. However, a deeper truth in the poem is that human beings exist in the very heart of nature, squirming through its living splendor that is splendorous only because all that lives must die. Being immersed in precious, continually transforming nature, part of nature—not above it, not below it, not standing off to the side—is remarkable indeed.

This book has shown that Issa's vision of humanity is a compassionate vision of social divisons mattering less than what people hold in common: a loving excitement for nature that begins in early childhood and continues throughout life for those lucky adults who manage to learn, as Issa did, how to access their open, accepting, nonjudgemntal childlike consciousness. However, people also have in common the power of voraciously self-serving egos—a power that the founder of Jōdoshinshū Buddhism, Shinran, declared to be inescapable. Everyone desires; everyone sins; everyone fails. This aspect of being human, a recurring theme for Issa, perfectly aligns with the tenets of his Pure Land faith. Only by relying on Amida's Other Power, originating from beyond the ego, can a person take the final step to complete the process of becoming truly human: surrendering to a higher (or, perhaps more accurately) inner power, thus achieving the enlightenment that is his or her birthright.

Issa's famous streak of iconoclasm can be understood to form part of a program to see through the artificial differences that divide people and to discover the natural connections and natural sameness that binds them together. Farmers, samurai, priests, courtesans, artisans, merchants, beggars, crossroads singers, Twelfth Month singers, Ainu outcastes, samisen-plucking geisha, and massive, colliding sumo wresters—again and again in Issa's haiku—reveal a common humanity of struggle and suffering, of adherence to art and beauty, of joy in nature, of love of family, of grieving at loss. Even the pickpockets working at a temple where pilgrims chant their gratitude for Amida's saving vow—though possibly unaware of this fact—can be liberated, one day, by that vow . . . or so Issa implies.

Early in his career, we have seen, he adopted the persona of a wandering beggar and priest of Haikai Temple, but soon, by his thirties, he added to this image that of an old man, losing his teeth, contemplating his wrinkles, and keenly sensing the Buddhist value of transience. His own life, like the lives of the myriad people sketched in his poetic notebooks, gradually came to embody the Buddha's teaching that all is fleeting, that nothing abides. Ultimately, to be born human for Issa means to return, perhaps in one's old age, to the condition of a newborn baby to see through the fictions of ego and social hierarchy (the latter being, in essence, simply a combative multiplicity of egos) in order to understand that we are essentially no different than puppies, than cats, than flies . . . than each other.

A vision of humanity inextricably connected to all creatures and living things on Planet Earth is especially relevant today, at a time when our delicately balanced ecosystem is threatened by the greed of egos swollen so huge that they will never be satisfied, this side of death; they will devour and exploit and pillage with no thought of other people, no thought of future generations. This being the case, it may come as a comfort to readers that Issa's prognosis for our species appears to be a hopeful one. Where warriors once drenched fields with the blood of enemies that they could not recognize to be, essentially, themselves; sooner or later, Issa promises, the poppies again will grow. And if the poppies win, we will.

Appendix: MORE PEOPLE PORTRAITS BY ISSA

畠打が焼石積る夕べかな (1792; *IZ* 1.116)
hata uchi ga yakeishi tsumeru yūbe kana

the plowman stacks
volcanic rocks . . .
evening

畠打がうてば唸る霰かな (1794; *IZ* 1.647)
hata uchi ga uteba unaru arare kana

plowing the field—
the clatter
of hailstones

青梅や餓鬼大将が肌ぬいで (1795; *IZ* 1.425)
aoume ya gaki-daishō ga hada nuide

green plums—
the baddest of bad boys
bare-chested

下枝に子も口真ねや閑古鳥 (1803; *IZ* 1.347)
shita eda ni ko mo kuchi mane ya kankodori

on a low branch
a child's imitation . . .
mountain cuckoo

桑つむや負れし柿も手を出して (1803; *IZ* 1.176)
kuwa tsumu ya owareshi kaki mo te wo dashite

picking mulberry leaves—
the baby on her back
stretches a hand

老僧のけばけばしさよ春の山 (1804; *IZ* 1.98)
rōsō no kebakebashisa yo haru no yama

the old priest
in his fancy clothes . . .
spring mountain

万歳のまかり出たよ親子連 (1804; *IZ* 1.47)
manzai no makari ideta yo oyako-zure

the begging actors
pay a visit . . .
parents and children

田の人の笠に糞してかへる雁 (1804; *IZ* 1.151)
ta no hito no kasa ni hako shite kaeru kari

pooping on the farmer's
umbrella-hat
the goose departs

膝の児の指始梅の花 (1804; *IZ* 1.193)
hiza no ko no yubisashi hajime ume no hana

the lap-baby's
first pointing . . .
plum blossoms

卯の花や葬の真似する子ども達 (1804; *IZ* 1.422)
u no hana ya sō no mane suru kodomotachi

deutzia blossoms—
the children play
funeral

朝露の朝顔売るやあら男 (1805; *IZ* 1.565)
asa tsuyu no asagao uru ya araotoko

selling morning-glories
wet with morning dew . . .
a tough character

金のなる木のめはりけりえたが家 (1805; *IZ* 1.188)
kane no naru ki no me hari keri eta ga ie

turning gold
budding branches overspread . . .
outcaste's home

売飯に夕木がらしのかかりけり (1806; *IZ* 1.631)
urimeshi ni yū kogarashi no kakari keri

over the vendor's cooked food
evening's
winter wind

春風に箸を掴んで寝る子哉 (1807; *IZ* 1.75)
haru kaze ni hashi wo tsukande neru ko kana

in spring's breeze
clutching chopsticks
the sleeping child

御僧の其後見へぬつぎ木哉 (1807; *IZ* 1.119)
on sō no sono nochi mienu tsugiki kana

the blessed priest
won't see it in his next life . . .
grafted tree

我塚もやがて頼むぞ鉢敲 (1807; *IZ* 1.662)
waga tsuka mo yagate tanomu zo hachi tataki

my grave too
will soon need his prayer . . .
a monk beats his bowl

子供等が鹿と遊ぶや萩の花 (1808; *IZ* 1.572)
kodomora ga shika to asobu ya hagi no hana

children play
with the deer
bush clover blooming

深草の鶉鳴けりばばが糊 (1809; *IZ* 1.525)
fuku kusa no uzura naki keri baba ga nori

in deep grass
a quail sings . . .
grandma starches clothes

畠打の顔から暮るつくば山 (1809; *IZ* 1.116)
hata uchi no kao kara kururu tsukuba yama

a plowman facing
sunset . . .
Mount Tsukuba

ちる木の葉渡世念仏通りけり (1810; *IZ* 1.729)
chiru ki no ha tosei nembutsu tōri keri

leaves falling—
a prayer-chanting monk
passes by

迎へ火をおもしろがりし子供哉 (1810; *IZ* 1.492)
mukaebi wo omoshirogarishi kodomo kana

delighted by bonfires
for the dead . . .
children

植る田やけふもはらはら帰る雁 (1811; *IZ* 1.327)
ueru ta ya kyō mo hara-hara kaeru kari

rice planting—
today too, traveling geese
flutter down

秋行や沢庵番のうしろから (1811; *IZ* 1.447)
aki yuku ya takuan ban no ushiro kara

autumn departs
trailing the pickled radish
vendor

万ざいや門に居ならぶ鳩雀　(1811; *IZ* 1.47)
manzai ya kado ni inarabu hato suzume

begging actors at the gate—
pigeons and sparrows
in a row

夕顔の花で洟かむ娘かな　(1812; *IZ* 1.391)
yūgao no hana de hana kamu musume kana

blowing her snot
on the moonflower . . .
a young girl

みどり子や御箸いただくけさの春　(1812; *IZ* 1.26)
midori ko ya o-hashi itadaku kesa no haru

the baby given chopsticks
digs in . . .
spring's first morning

有明や梅にも一ッ鉢たたき　(1813; *IZ* 1.662)
ariake ya ume ni mo hitotsu hachi tataki

at dawn by the plum tree
there's one too . . .
a monk beats his bowl

子どもらが遊ぶ程ずつやくの哉 (1813; *IZ* 1.115)
kodomora ga asobu hodo-zutsu yaku no kana

the children
make it a playground . . .
burnt field

柳からももんぐわとて出る子哉 (1813; *IZ* 1.239)
yanagi kara momonguwa tote deru ko kana

from the willow
a ghost attacks!
the child

ちりめんの猿を抱く子よ丸雪ちる (1813; *IZ* 1.648)
chirimen no saru wo daku ko yo arare chiru

the child hugs
her cloth monkey . . .
hailstorm

わんぱくが仕業ながらも雪仏 (1813; *IZ* 1.695)
wanpaku ga shiwaza nagara mo yuki-botoke

naughty child—
instead of his chores
a snow Buddha

霰ちれくくり枕を負ふ子ども (1813; *IZ* 1.647)
arare chire kukurimakura woo u kodomo

fall, hailstones!
with pillow on his head
a child

古郷や梅干婆々が梅の花 (1814; *IZ* 1.198)
furusato ya umeboshi baba ga ume no hana

my home village—
a wrinkled old woman's
plum blossoms

負た子が先へ指さすわかな哉 (1814; *IZ* 1.51)
outta ko ga saki e yubi sasu wakana kana

the child on her back
points them out first . . .
New Year's herbs

ちさい子がきせる加へて刈穂哉 (1814; *IZ* 1.578)
chisai ko ga kiseru kuwaete kariho kana

a small child
chews on a pipe . . .
they harvest the rice

はつ雪やなむきえ僧の朝の声　(1814; *IZ* 1.637)
hatsu yuki ya namu kiesō no asa no koe

first snow—
a priest chants
his morning prayer

畠打の真似して歩く烏哉　(1814; *IZ* 1.117)
hata uchi no mane shite aruku karasu kana

mocking the farmer
plowing, the strutting
crow

涼しさや畠掘っても湯のけぶり　(1814; *IZ* 1.390)
suzushisa ya hatake hotte mo yu no keburi

cool air—
even for the dirt farmer
hot bath steam

木がくれや大念仏で田を植る　(1814; *IZ* 1.327)
kogakure ya ōnembutsu de ta wo ueru

hidden in trees
praising Amida Buddha . . .
rice planter

負た子が花ではやすや茶つみ唄 (1815; *IZ* 1.113)
ōta ko ga hana de hayasu ya cha tsumi uta

the child on her back
beats time with a flower . . .
tea-picking song

蕗の葉にいわしを配る田植哉 (1816; *IZ* 1.327)
fuki no ha ni iwashi wo kubaru taue kana

sardines served
in butterbur leaves . . .
planting rice

昼飯をぶらさげて居るかがし哉 (1816; *IZ* 1.510)
hiru meshi wo burasagete iru kagashi kana

the farmer's lunch
dangles . . .
on the scarecrow

木がらしや餌蒔の跡をおふ烏 (1816; *IZ* 1.632)
kogarashi ya emaki no ato wo ou karasu

winter wind—
behind the farmer sowing seeds
a crow

尿をやる子にあれあれと桜哉 (1816; *IZ* 1.230)
shito wo yaru ko ni are-are to sakura kana

a child pissing
"Look! Look!"
cherry blossoms

涼風の吹木へ縛る我子哉 (1816; *IZ* 1.255)
suzukaze no fuku ki e shibaru waga ko kana

tied to the tree
where cool wind blows
my child

僧正の天窓で折し氷柱哉 (1816; *IZ* 1.612)
sōjō no atama de orishi tsurara kana

using his head
the high priest breaking
icicles

大門や涼がてらの草むしり (1816; *IZ* 1.322)
daimon ya suzumi ga tera no kusa mushiri

great temple gate—
in the cool air a monk
plucks grass

しんしんと心底寒し新坊主 (1817; *IZ* 1.608)
shin-shin to shinsoko samushi shin bōzu

down to the bone
bitter cold . . .
the novice priest

畠打や尾上の松を友として (1817; *IZ* 1.117)
hata uchi ya onoe no matsu wo tomo to shite

plowing the field
he keeps the mountain ridge pine
company

おさなごや尿やりながら梅の花 (1817; *IZ* 1.200)
osanago ya shito yari nagara ume no hana

little child—
while Mama helps him pee-pee
plum blossoms

僧正もほた火仲間の座とり哉 (1817; *IZ* 1.708)
sōjō mo hotabi nakama no za tori kana

a cozy wood fire—
the high priest also
takes a seat

ちさい子がたばこ吹也麦の秋 (1817; *IZ* 1.406)
chisai ko ga tabako fuku nari mugi no aki

a little child
smoking a pipe . . .
ripened barley

春風や供の娘の小脇差 (1818; *IZ* 1.78)
harukaze ya tomo no musume no ko wakizashi

spring breeze—
the little servant girl
has a short sword

小坊主が子におしへけり天の川 (1818; *IZ* 1.449)
ko bōzu ga ko ni oshie keri ama no kawa

a little boy
shows another child . . .
Milky Way

雪解や貧乏町の痩せ子達 (1818; *IZ* 1.97)
yuki-doke ya bimbō machi no yase kodachi

snow melting—
the thin children
of the slum

いとこ雛孫雛と名の付合ふ (1818; *IZ* 1.107)
itoko hina mago hina to na no tsuki tamau

"Cousin Doll"
and "Grandchild Doll"
she names them

継っ子や昼寝仕事に蚤拾ふ (1818; *IZ* 1.307)
mamakko ya hirune shigoto ni nomi hirou

siesta work
for the stepchild . . .
picking brother's fleas[54]

是程のぼたんと仕かたする子哉 (1818; *IZ* 1.394)
kore hodo no botan to shikata suru ko kana

"The peony is this big!"
the child's arms
outstretched

小島にも畠打也鳴雲雀 (1818; *IZ* 1.144)
kojima ni mo hatake utsunari naku hibari

on a tiny island, too
plowing
to the lark's song

祝ひ日や白い僧達白い蝶 (1818; *IZ* 1.171)
iwai-bi ya shiroi sōdachi shiroi chō

festival day—
white robed monks
and a white butterfly

士の供を連たる御犬哉 (1818; *IZ* 1.745)
samurai no tomo wo tsuretaru o-inu kana

joining the samurai's
company . . .
Sir Dog

舞は蝶三弦流布の小村也 (1818; *IZ* 1.172)
mau wa chō samisen rufu no ko mura nari

butterfly dance—
someone plays samisen
in the little village

小盲や右も左もむら時雨 (1818; *IZ* 1.627)
ko mekura ya migi wa hidari mo mura shigure

a blind child—
to his right, to his left
steady winter rain

正月やえたの玄関も梅の花 (1818; *IZ* 1.25)
shōgatsu ya eta no genkan mo ume no hana

First Month—
even at the outcaste's porch
plum blossoms

初瓜を引とらまえて寝た子哉 (1819; *IZ* 1.414)
hatsu uri wo hittoramaete neta ko kana

first melon of the season
in her grasp . . .
sleeping child

露の玉つまんで見たるわらべ哉 (1819; *IZ* 1.480)
tsuyu no tama tsumande mitaru warabe kana

trying to pinch
a bead of dew . . .
a child

餅搗が隣へ来たと云子哉 (1819; *IZ* 1.674)
mochi tsuki ga tonari e kita to iu ko nari

"The rice cake man
is next door!"
the child announces

大根引拍子にころり小僧哉 (1819; *IZ* 1.726)
daiko hiku hyōshi ni korori kozō kana

yanking a radish
taking a tumble . . .
little boy

ざくざくと雪かき交ぜて田打哉 (1819; *IZ* 1.116)
zaku-zaku to yuki kakimazete ta uchi kana

crunch! crunch!
plowing the rice field
snow

そんじよそこここと青田のひいき哉 (1819; *IZ* 1.279)
sonji yo soko koko to aoda no hiiki kana

this or that green rice field?
each farmer
is biased

西方のはつ空拝む法師哉 (1819; *IZ* 1.33)
saihō no hatsu-zora ogamu hōshi kana

westward he prays
to the year's first sky . . .
priest

鰯めせめせとや泣子負ながら (1819; *IZ* 1.551)
iwashi mese mese to ya naku ko oi nagara

"Get your sardines!"
she cries, a crying baby
on her back

三絃に鳴つく許り千鳥哉 (1819; *IZ* 1.718)
samisen ni nakitsuku bakari chidori kana

begging her to play
her samisen . . .
plovers

里の子や杓子で作る雪の山 (1820; *IZ* 1.694)
sato no ko ya shakushi de tsukuru yuki no yama

the village child
builds it with a spoon . . .
Snow Mountain

春雨や猫におどりをおしえる子 (1820; *IZ* 1.73)
harusame ya neko ni odori wo oshieru ko

spring rain—
a child gives a dance lesson
to the cat

蚕医者蚕医者する娘かな (1820; *IZ* 1.176)
kaiko isha kaiko isha suru musume kana

playing doctor
for the silkworms . . .
little girl

朝霜やしかも子どものお花売 (1820; *IZ* 1.652)
asa shimo ya shikamo kodomo no o-hana uri

morning frost—
yet still a child sells
temple flowers

腕にも露がおく也御茶売 (1820; *IZ* 1.481)
kaina ni mo tsuyu ga oku nari ocha uri

even on his arms
dewdrops
the tea seller

卯の花や子供の作る土だんご (1821; *IZ* 1.423)
u no hana ya kodomo no tsukuru tsuchi dango

deutzia in bloom
the children make
mud-dumplings

小坊主が転げくらする菫哉 (1821; *IZ* 1.185)
ko bōzu ga koroge kurasuru sumire kana

the little boy
tumbling all day . . .
violets

人の世や山の上でも田植うた (1821; *IZ* 1.328)
hito no yo ya yama no ue demo taue uta

world of man—
even atop a mountain
rice planters singing

松を友鶴を友なる田打哉 (1821; *IZ* 1.116)
matsu wo tomo tsuru wo tomo naru ta uchi kana

friend of the pine
friend of the crane . . .
he plows his field

温泉のけぶる際より田植哉 (1821; *IZ* 1.328)
onsen no keburu kiwa yori taue kana

touched by
the hot spring's steam . . .
planting rice

寝並んで小蝶と猫と和尚哉 (1821; *IZ* 1.173)
ne narande ko chō to neko to oshō kana

sleeping in a row—
little butterfly, cat
high priest

老僧が塵拾ひけり苔の花 (1821; *IZ* 1.409)
rōsō ga chiri hiroi keri koke no hana

the old priest
picks off the dust . . .
moss blossoms

武士やいひわけ云てから御慶 (1821; *IZ* 1.40)
samurai ya iiwake iute kara gyokei

a samurai—
after an apology
a "Happy New Year!"

武士村やからたち垣の年始状 (1821; *IZ* 1.40)
bushi mura ya karatachi kaki no nenshijō

samurai street—
over the quince hedge
"Happy New Year!"

念仏も三絃に引く祭り哉 (1821; *IZ* 1.280)
nembutsu mo samisen ni hiku matsuri kana

praising Buddha too
with her samisen . . .
festival

母親を霜よけにして寝た子哉 (1821; *IZ* 1.697)
haha oya wo shimoyoke ni shite neta ko kana

Mother
is the frost-guard . . .
sleeping child

背たけの箕をかぶる子やはつ時雨 (1822; *IZ* 1.623)
seitake no mi wo kaburu ko ya hatsu shigure

with a winnow the boy
covers his head . . .
first winter rain

凧の糸引とらまへて寝る子哉 (1822; *IZ* 1.46)
tako no ito hikitoramaete neru ko kana

clinging to the kite's
string . . .
the sleeping child

雛達に咄しかける子ども哉 (1822; *IZ* 1.108)
hina-dachi ni hanashi shikakeru kodomo kana

giving her dolls
a good talking-to . . .
the child

しら露としらぬ子どもが仏かな (1822; *IZ* 1.483)
shira tsuyu to shiranu kodomo ga hotoke kana

the child unaware
of the silver dewdrops
a Buddha

赤足袋を手におっぱめる子ども哉 (1822; *IZ* 1.690)
aka tabi wo te ni oppameru kodomo kana

trying the red socks
on his hands . . .
the child

春風に肩衣かけて御供かな (1822; *IZ* 1.78)
harukaze ni kataginu kakete o-tomo kana

in spring breeze
his stole billowing . . .
a monk comes too

伴僧が手習す也わか葉陰 (1822; *IZ* 1.418)
bansō ga tenaraisu nari wakaba kage

the monk practices
calligraphy
in the shade of new leaves

花売の花におくや露の玉 (1822; *IZ* 1.483)
hanauri no hana ni oku ya tsuyu no tama

on the flower vendor's
flowers . . .
pearls of dew

沼の蓮葉さへ花さへ売られけり (1822; *IZ* 1.399)
numa no hasu ha sae hana sae urare keri

they even sell
the swamp's lotuses . . .
leaf and blossom

松に腰かけて土民も扇哉 (1823; *IZ* 1.311)
matsu ni koshi kakete domin mo ōgi kana

also left hanging
in the pine . . .
the farmer's paper fan

武士町やしんかんとして明の春 (1823; *IZ* 1.27)
bushi machi ya shinkan to shite ake no haru

the samurai street
perfectly silent
spring's first dawn

春風や武士も吹るる女坂 (1823; *IZ* 1.79)
haru kaze ya bushi mo fukaruru onnazaka

spring breeze—
even a samurai is blown
down the slope

声々や子どもの交じる浜千鳥 (1824; *IZ* 1.719)
koe-goe ya kodomo no majiru hama chidori

an uproar on the beach—
children
and plovers

梅さくや羽織を着せる小人形 (1824; *IZ* 1.205)
ume saku ya haori wo kiseru ko ningyō

plum blossoms—
the child puts a coat
on her doll

早乙女におぶさって寝る小てふ哉 (1824; *IZ* 1.328)
saotome ni obusatte neru ko chō kana

rice-planting girl—
on her back a butterfly
sleeps

年玉や懐の子も手々をして (1824; *IZ* 1.41)
toshi-dama ya futokoro no ko mo te-te wo shite

New Year's present—
the nursing baby reaches
with little hands

畠打や鍬でをしへる寺の松 (1824; *IZ* 1.118)
hata uchi ya kuwa de oshieru tera no matsu

with his hoe the farmer
shows the way . . .
temple pine

小乞食の唄三絃や夏の月 (1824; *IZ* 1.273)
ko kojiki no uta samisen ya natsu no tsuki

the beggar child
plucks and sings . . .
summer moon

卯の花や子らが蛙の墓参 (1825; *IZ* 1.424)
u no hana ya kora ga kawazu no hakamairi

deutzia blossoms—
the children visit
the frog's grave

七夕やよい子持てる乞食村 (1826; *IZ* 1.499)
tanabata ya yoi ko motteru kojiki machi

Tanabata Night—
the well-behaved children
of beggar-town

桃咲や犬にまたがる悪太郎 (? ; *IZ* 1.236)
momo saku ya inu ni matagaru akutarō

peach blossoms—
riding a dog
the naughty boy

ちさい子が草背負けり五月雨 (? ; *IZ* 1.262)
chisai ko ga kusa seoi keri satsuki ame

a small child
a bundle of hay on his back . . .
Fifth Month rain

末の子や御墓参りの箒持　(? ; *IZ* 1.492)
sue no ko ya o-haka mairi no hōki mochi

the youngest child
on the grave visit
brings the broom

昼顔にふんどし晒す小僧かな　(? ; *IZ* 1.390)
hirugao ni fundoshi sarasu kozō kana

in day flowers
airing out his loincloth . . .
little boy

里の子の袂からちる桜かな　(? ; *IZ* 1.234)
sato no ko no tamoto kara chiru sakura kana

trickling from
a village child's sleeve . . .
cherry blossoms

つぐら子の口ばたなめる小てふ哉　(? ; *IZ* 1.175)
tsugura ko no kuchi-bata nameru ko chō kana

baby in a basket—
licking the edge of her mouth
little butterfly

入道が綻ぬふや春の雨 (? ; *IZ* 1.74)
nyūdō ga hokorobi nuu ya haru no ame

the priest is mending
a rip . . .
spring rain

春風や歩行ながらの御法談 (? ; *IZ* 1.79)
haru kaze ya aruki nagara no ōhōdan

spring breeze—
the priest gives his sermon
walking along

洗たくの婆々へ柳の夕なびき (? ; *IZ* 1.242)
sentaku no baba e yanagi no yū nabiki

to the old woman
doing laundry, the evening
willow bows

NOTES

1. Kobayashi Issa, *Issa zenshū* (Nagano: Shinano Mainichi Shimbunsha, 1979) 6.31. All texts from Issa are from the nine-volume *Issa zenshū* (hereafter *IZ*). Here and henceforth, English translations of Japanese are my own unless otherwise designated.

2. Fay Aoyagi made me aware of this possible reading of *naka-naka ni* at a meeting of the Haiku Society of America in Hot Springs, Arkansas, on 5 November 2016. A dictionary of Old Japanese, the *Kogo daijiten*, corroborates Fay's insight; in olden days *naka naka ni* could mean "not satisfied and not dissatisfied": a halfway or in-between state (1,206). I'm indebted to Fay and to all the attendees of the Hot Springs conference, who gave me useful feedback when I presented some of the key arguments of this book.

3. It was written before the deaths of his first four children: losses that certainly added to the poet's sense of the fragile preciousness of human life. However, Issa appreciated this preciousness—as suggested by this and other haiku—long before having and losing children.

4. In this book I follow the traditional Japanese way of counting age, according to which a child is one at birth and gains a year with each New Year's Day. Issa was born on the fifth day of Fifth Month, 1763: June 15 on the Western calendar. That next New Year's Day, he turned two—though Western parents would have described him as only eight months old. This is why, though he was officially three years old when his mother died in 1765, by Western reckoning he

would have been just over two and a half. Similarly, he left home at age fourteen (Japanese reckoning), at a time that he was only approaching his thirteenth birthday by the Western standard.

5. This theme is investigated in the companion book to this one: *Issa and the Meaning of Animals*. See especially Chapter 4: Shinto and Buddhist Animals.

6. Much of this chapter appeared as an essay, "Becoming a Child: Issa's Poetic Consciousness."

7. At a meeting of the Haiku Society of America in Winter Park, Florida on 16 May 2015, Stanford M. Forrester elaborated on Keroauc's childlike approach in a talk titled, "The Haiku Be-Bop of Jack Kerouac and the Beats."

8. In an earlier haiku (1810), a child clutches plum blossoms tightly (*IZ* 1.195). By making the child lost in the haiku of 1814, Issa adds emotional power to the image.

9. In this case the child in question is not Issa's own, unless the haiku is written from a memory; his two year-old daughter Sato died earlier that year.

10. This undated haiku might either be a precursor or revision of one of 1816:

> 凧抱たなりですやすや寝たりけり (1816; *IZ* 1.46)
> *tako daita nari de suya-suya netari keri*
>
> hugging his kite
> he sleeps
> deep and calm

11. A related example is this haiku of 1821:

稲妻をとらまへたがる子ども哉 (*IZ* 1.484)
inazuma wo toramaetagaru kodomo kana

trying to catch
the lightning bolt . . .
a child

12. In an undated version Issa begins this haiku with the phrase, "blooming plum" (*ume saku ya* 梅さくや); *IZ* 1.197.

13. This Japanese word was used as a formal, humble signing-off expression in old-style letters, equivalent to "Yours Truly."

14. For a discussion of Issa's haiku about *mukudori*, see my book, *Pure Land Haiku*, Chapter 1: "*UNSUI*: Cloud-Water Wanderer."

15. In this way Issa reduces its syllable count from six to four, so that with the addition of the "cutting" particle *ya* it achieves the five-syllable ideal for a haiku's first phrase.

16. *Daijirin Japanese Dictionary* 2nd Edition, qtd. in "Mottainai," *Wikipedia*. In recent times environmentalists have used the word to express shame at wasting natural resources.

17. See "Flower Power: Issa's Revolution" (2004).

18. According to volume 1 of Issa's complete works, this haiku was written in 1824. However, it appears in an 1823 entry in volume 4; see *IZ* 1.387 and 4.430.

19. One *ri* is 2.44 miles. The mountain farmer's field is "two or three" *ri* way: 4.88 to 7.32 miles. *Yamaudo*, literally, a "mountain person," also can signify a hermit.

20. In addition to the historical Buddha, Gautama, several Buddhas were important in Issa's Japan, such as the Universal Buddha of the Lotus Sutra and Amida Buddha, a liberating "Other Power" in Pure Land Buddhism.

21. *Kogo daijiten* 430.

22. See Issa's discussion of Shinran's doctrine in *Oraga haru*; *IZ* 6.135-36. I analyze this discussion in close detail in *Pure Land Haiku: The Art of Priest Issa*, Chapter 7: "*NEMBUTSU, TARIKI*: Prayer and Grace."

23. I use the terms "monk" and "priest" interchangeably when translating Issa's words denoting Buddhist clerics.

24. See my discussion of this scene in *Issa and the Meaning of Animals*, Chapter 2: "Anthropomorphism or Realism?"

25. For example:

> さをしかや社壇に角を奉る (1824; *IZ* 1.125)
> *saoshika ya shadan ni tsuno wo tatematsuru*
>
> on the shrine's altar
> the buck offers
> his antlers

I discuss this and similar haiku in *Issa and the Meaning of Animals*, Chapter 4: "Shinto and Buddhist Animals."

26. 閑さや岩にしみ入る蝉の声 (1689; Bashō 1.276)
shizukasa ya iwa ni shimi-iru semi no koe

> tranquility –
> seeping into solid rock
> cicada song

27. A famous example is Issa's haiku about snow melting in a village, previously quoted:

雪とけて村一ぱいの子ども哉 (1814; *IZ* 1.95)
yuki tokete mura ippai no kodomo kana

snow melting
the village brimming over . . .
with children!

28. In the poem Issa shortens *nembutsu* to *nebutsu*, reducing the number of sound units from four to three and thereby fitting the normal 5-7-5 pattern of Japanese haiku.

29. The bird might be a nightingale, in light of several other haiku by Issa that equate the songs of these birds with the Lotus Sutra, for example:

信濃なる鶯も法ほけ経哉 (1811; *IZ* 1.132)
shinano naru uguisu mo hohokekyō kana

even the nightingale
of Shinano sings it . . .
Lotus Sutra

30. Holly, normally pronounced *hiiragi*, is pronounced *hiragi* in this case to fit the 5-7-5 pattern of sound units.

31. See my essay, "Flower Power: Issa's Revolution" (2004).

32. This is much like Anubis of the ancient Egyptian underworld weighing deceased people's hearts against the feather of Truth (*ma'at*).

33. It is also possible to imagine that the samurai has been derelict in his duty and has had his topknot forcibly removed

by his lord, but I feel, in the historical context of the peaceful early nineteenth century, this dramatic interpretation of the haiku probably would have been unlikely for Issa's original readers. One Japanese advisor, Professor Shokan Tadashi Kondo, feels strongly that the samurai is becoming a Buddhist monk.

34. Although female samurai existed, there is no evidence in any of his poems that Issa is referring to such women.

35. According to my Japanese advisor Shinji Ogawa, this plant, "pheasant's eye," blooms in early spring, around New Year's Day in the old Japanese calendar.

36. Literally, he does it in his *sanzun no mune*: "three *sun* heart," a *sun* equaling approximately 1.2 inches. Issa's "heart" of three *sun* (around 3.6 inches) isn't his anatomical heart but rather the heart of his mental activities, in this case, mental arithmetic.

37. This is quite unlike the English poem, "The Chimney Sweeper," written by Issa's contemporary, William Blake in *Songs of Innocence* (1789).

38. 浄はりや梅盗む手が先うつる (1812; *IZ* 1.197)
    jōhari ya ume nusumu te ga mazu utsuru

    in hell's mirror
    the plum-blossom thief's
    reflection

39. Bashō's famous poems about a frog jumping into an old pond and about a crow on a bare autumn branch present the English translator with a similar judgement call. Most translators choose to imagine and depict just one frog, one crow, for this seems sufficient. However, there have been

contrarian translators who have multiplied the frogs and crows, I think, unnecessarily.

40. The journal was published in 1852, commemorating the twenty-fifth anniversary of Issa's death, according to the old Japanese calendar (though in the Western calendar, 1853 would be the twenty-fifth anniversary of his passing). Hyōkai Shisanjin wrote the first postscript, dated 1851; Seian Saiba wrote the second, undated postscript. See *IZ* 6. 157; 165.

41. See Plate 5 of Richard Illing, *Japanese Erotic Art and the Life of the Courtesan*.

42. Issa shortens *jōro* to *joro* in the haiku, in order to achieve a 5-7-5 pattern of sound units.

43. *Kogo daijiten* (Shogakukan 1983) 1671.

44. *Kogo daijiten* (Shogakukan 1983) 167.

45.　おれとして白眼くらする蛙かな (1819; *IZ* 1.162)
 ore to shite niramikura suru kawazu kana

 locked in a staring contest
 me . . .
 and a frog

46. He was assisted by his Japanese advisor Emiko Sakurai; *The Haiku Handbook* 18.

47. The word *kotsujiki* is the old pronunciation of the word "beggar" in this haiku. However, my Japanese advisor, Sakuo Nakamura, who grew up in the same language area as Issa, feels confident that Issa would have pronounced the word, *konjiki*.

48. Though undated, this is an early haiku written in the 1790s.

49. See my essay, "The Haiku Mind: Pure Land Buddhism and Issa" (2008).

50. *Kyōgyōshinshō* 3.

51. *Kogo daijiten* 264.

52. Incidentally, laws prohibiting the abandonment of the elderly were enacted only after fifth shogun Tsunayoshi Tokugawa (1646-1709), a Buddhist, decreed the death penalty for cruelty to dogs. The dogs of Japan received legal protection before the nation's old people did (Prasol 99).

53. Issa puns delightfully with two meanings of *hana*: "blossom" (花) and "snot" (洟).

54. The word "brother" has been added to clarify the scene in light of Issa's biography.

WORKS CITED

Blyth, R. H. *Haiku*. Tokyo: Hokuseido, 1949-1952; rpt. 1981-1982 [reset paperback edition]. 4 vols. Print.

Carhart-Harris, Robin. "The Entropic Brain: A Theory of Conscious States Informed by Neuroimaging Research with Psychedelic Drugs." *Frontiers in Human Neuroscience*. 3 February 2014. Web.

Cholley, Jean. *En village de miséreux: Choix de poèmes de Kobayashi Issa*. Paris: Gallimard, 1996. Print.

Cunningham, Don. *Taiho-Jutsu: Law and Order in the Age of the Samurai*. Boston, Rutland Vermont and Tokyo: Tuttle Publishing, 2004. Print.

Deal, William E. *Handbook to Life in Medieval and Early Modern Japan*. New York: Facts on File, 2006. Print.

Ekken Kaibara. *Onna Daigaku: A Treasure Box of Women's Learning*. Ed. L. Cranmer-Byng and S. A. Kapadia. Weston-super-Mare, United Kingdom: Nezu Press, 2010. Print.

Falkman, Kai. *Understanding Haiku: A Pyramid of Meaning*. Winchester, VA: Red Moon Press, 2002. Print.

Forrester, Stanford D. "The Haiku Be-Bop of Jack Kerouac and the Beats." Haiku Society of America Quarterly Meeting. Winter Park, Florida. 16 May 2015. Lecture.

Greve, Gabi. "December Singers (*sekizoro*)." *World Kigo Database*. Accessed 18 November 2016. Web.

Groemer, Gerald. "Who Benefits? Religious Practice, Blind Women '(Goze), Harugoma,' and 'Manzai.'" *Japanese Journal of Religious Studies* 41.2 (2014): 347-86. Print.

Henderson, Harold G. *An Introduction to Haiku*. New York: Doubleday, 1958. Print.

Illing, Richard. *Japanese Erotic Art and the Life of the Courtesan* (New York: Gallery Books, rpt. 1983). Print.

Kerouac, Jack. *The Dharma Bums*. New York: Penguin, 1976. Print.

Kobayashi Masafune. *Issa to onnatachi*. Tokyo: Sanwa, 2004. Print.

Kobayashi Issa. *Issa zenshū (IZ)*. Ed. Kobayashi Keiichirō. 9 vols. Nagano: Shinano Mainichi Shimbunsha, 1976-79. Print.

---. *The Year of My Life: A Translation of Issa's Oraga Haru*. Tran. Yuasa Nobuyuki. 2nd ed. Berkeley: Univ. of California Press, 1972. Print.

Kogo daijiten. Tokyo: Shogakukan 1983. Print.

Lanoue, David G. "Becoming a Child: Issa's Poetic Consciousness." *Modern Haiku* 46.3 (Autumn 2015): 23-33.

---. "Flower Power: Issa's Revolution." *Simply Haiku* 2.2 (March-April 2004). Web. Reprinted in the online Canadian journal, *WAH* (Spring 2014). Web.

---. *Issa and the Meaning of Animals: A Buddhist Poet's Perspective*. New Orleans: HaikuGuy.com, 2014.

---. "The Haiku Mind: Pure Land Buddhism and Issa." *Eastern Buddhist* 39.2 (2008): 159-76. Print.

---. "The Poetic 'Ah!': Haiku and the Right Brain." *Simply Haiku* 5.2 (Summer 2007). Web. Reprinted in *Dust of Summers: The Red Moon Anthology of English-Language Haiku*. Ed. Jim Kacian. Winchester, VA. Red Moon Press, 2008. 147-54. Print.

---. *Pure Land Haiku: The Art of Priest Issa*. Reno, Nevada and Fukagawa-shi, Hokkaido: Buddhist Books International, 2004. Print.

Laozi. *Dao De Jing: A New-Millennium Translation*. Tran. David H. Li. Bethesda, Maryland: Premier Publishing Co., 2001. Print.

Maruyama Kazuhiko. *Issa haiku shū*. Tokyo: Iwanami Shoten, 1990; rpt. 1993. Print.

Matuso Bashō. Ed. Imoto Nōichi. *Matsuo Bashōshū*. Vol. 1. Tokyo: Shogakukan, 1995. Print.

---. *The Narrow Road to the Deep North and Other Travel Sketches*. Tran. Nobuyuki Yuasa. New York: Penguin 1981. Print.

"Mottainai." *Wikipedia*. Accessed 1 April 2016. Web.

Nouet, Noel. *The Shogun's City: A History of Tokyo*. Tran. John & Michele Mills. Sandgate, Folkstone England: Paul Norbury, 1990. Print.

Pollan, Michael. "The Trip Treatment." *The New Yorker*. 9 Feb. (2015): 36-47. Print.

Prasol, Alexander. *Modern Japan: Origins of the Mind; Japanese Traditions and Approaches to Contemporary Life*. London and Hackensack, New Jersey: World Scientific, 2010. Print.

Rouzer, Paul. "A Dream of Ruined Walls." *Simply Haiku* 4.2 (Summer 2006). Web.

Seigle, Cecilia Segawa. *Yoshiwara: The Glittering World of the Japanese Courtesan*. Honolulu: University of Hawaii Press, 1993. Print.

Shiu, H., & Stokes, L. "Buddhist Animal Release Practices: Historic, Environmental, Public Health and Economic Concerns." *Contemporary Buddhism* 9 (2008): 181-196. Print.

Shinran. *The* Kyōgyōshinshō: *The Collection of Passages Expounding the True Teaching, Living, Faith, and Realizing of the Pure Land*. Tran. D. T. Suzuki. Kyoto: Shinshu Otaniha, 1973. Print.

Sone Hiromi. "Prostitution and Public Authority in Early Modern Japan." Tran. Terashima Akiko and Anne Walthall. *Women and Class in Japanese History*. Eds. Tonomura Hitomi, Anne Walthall, and Wakita Haruko. Ann Arbor: Center for Japanese Studies, The University of Michigan, 1999. Print.

Stanley, Amy. *Selling Women: Prostitution, Markets, and the Household in Early Modern Japan*. Berkeley: University of California Press, 2012. Print.

Suzuki, D. T. *Shin Buddhism*. New York: Harper & Row, 1970. Print.

Ueda Makoto. *Dew on the Grass: The Life and Poetry of Kobayashi Issa*. Leiden/Boston: Brill, 2004. Print.

Walker, Brett L. *The Conquest of Ainu Lands: Ecology and Culture in Japanese Expansion, 1590-1800*. Berkeley: University of California Press, 2006. Print.

Yamamoto Tsunetomo. *Hagakuru: The Book of the Samurai*. Tran. William Scott Wilson. Tokyo and New York: Kodansha international, 1979. Print.

ABOUT THE AUTHOR

David G. Lanoue is a professor of English at Xavier University of Louisiana. He is a cofounder of the New Orleans Haiku Society, an associate member of the Haiku Foundation, and former President of the Haiku Society of America. His books include translations (*Cup-of-Tea Poems; Selected Haiku of Kobayashi Issa* and *The Distant Mountain: The Life and Haiku of Kobayashi Issa*), criticism (*Pure Land Haiku: The Art of Priest Issa* and *Issa and the Meaning of Animals: A Buddhist Poet's Perspective*), and a series of "haiku novels," including *Haiku Guy, Laughing Buddha, Haiku Wars, Frog Poet* and *Dewdrop World*. Some of his books have appeared in French, German, Spanish, Bulgarian, Serbian, and Japanese editions. He maintains *The Haiku of Kobayashi Issa* website, for which he translated 10,000 of Issa's haiku.

Made in the USA
San Bernardino, CA
17 September 2017